When the Truth Lies
By
Saoirse Durant

First paperback edition September 2023

Book cover design by Mandy Idema

ISBN 978-9-0903-7526-7 (paperback)
ASIN: B0CB74BN4G (ebook)

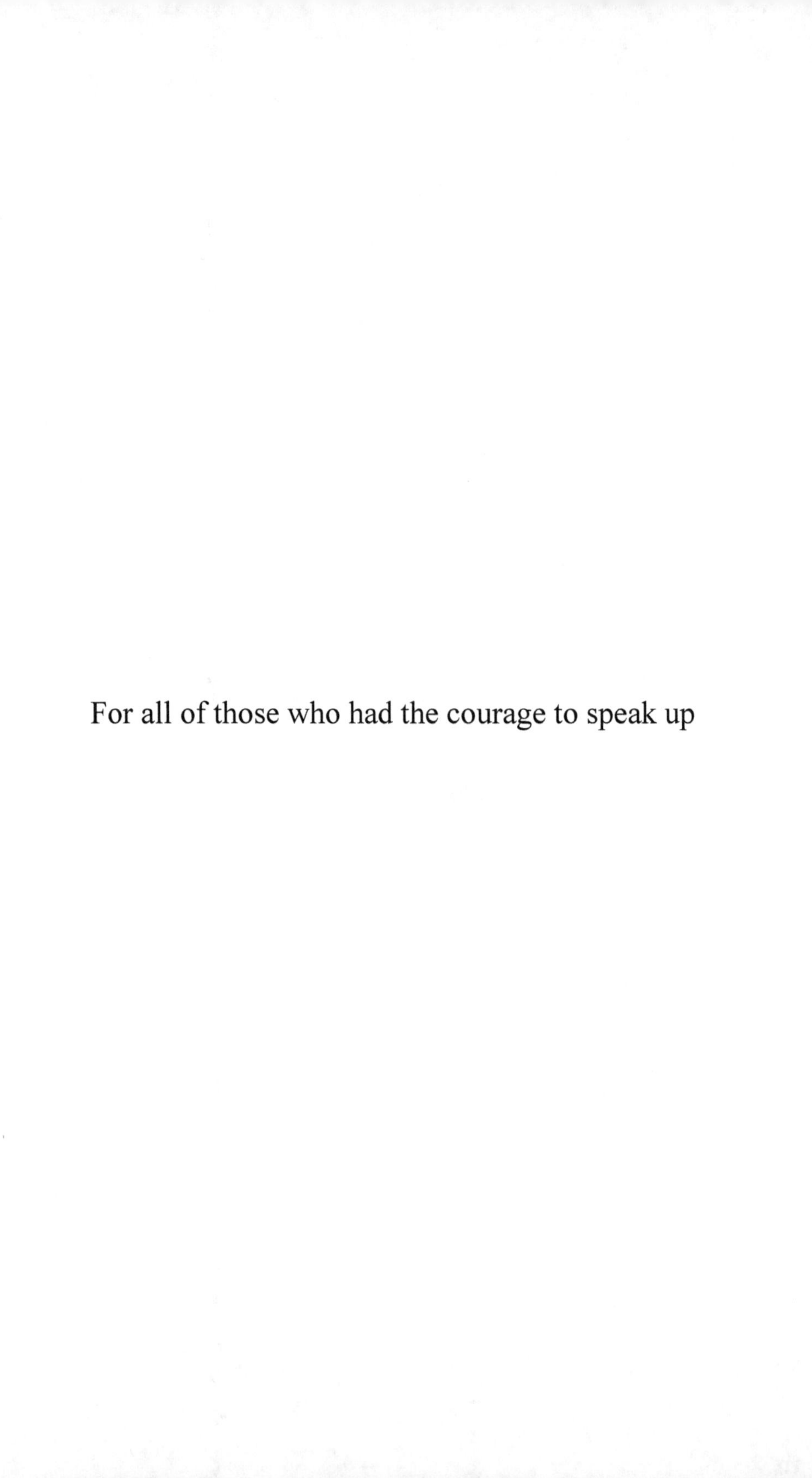

For all of those who had the courage to speak up

Preface

This book is not a factual retelling of someone's experience within the sect. The characters and the specific events described, to the best of my knowledge, do not exist and have not existed in real life. However, the story as written could potentially have happened. This is because it is based on a sect that does exist. Known as The Truth, The Way, The Friends and Workers, The Two-by-Twos, the sect has no official name, and yet somehow many different names.

Before we start, for anyone wanting to know more about the group as the book goes on, and looking for the facts, I would recommend these links below.

www.wikipedia.org/wiki/Two_by_Twos

www.tellingthetruth.info

I also want to give some trigger warnings with the book. I address some of the heavier issues that are problematic within the group, so there are mentions of child sexual abuse and abuse in general. If you are not in the right mindset, consider that this book may not be the best option for you right now. Look after yourself. If you are a victim of child or any type of sexual abuse, contact your local authorities if you have not already done so. For those victims who are/ were members of the organisation, there are resources on:

This website, advocates for the truth, also has an option for any wishing to donate to support survivors directly.

For further information on sexual abuse and abusers within the group, visit wings for truth.

Please be aware that this information is accurate as of when the book is published. The websites and other details may change.

Chapter One

They sat in a circle. In a house, on a hill, in the middle of everywhere. The house wasn't anything unusual, the people inside nothing special. Nobody spoke. There was a silence, but not your usual type of silence. This silence included a clock in the corner, making its voice heard with a predictable regularity.

Tick tock

Tick tock

Tick tock

It seemed to become the silence, something you could tune out if you weren't listening. But, if through some mistake you did accidentally tune in, you couldn't unhear it. It infiltrated your thoughts like a worm, wriggling its way around your head, becoming impossible to ignore.

Tick tock

Tick tock

There were, of course, the occasional sounds which suggested that these people in the circle were indeed people – a cough, someone clearing their throat, a small child shifting in their chair.

Tick tock

Tick tock

The silence was only broken when more people came to join the circle, some murmured greetings, some clipping of heels, and children chattering outside to be quieted instantly when they entered the room.

Tick tock

Tick tock

Tick tock

Five minutes later, the last family had settled. Drawing materials were delicately balanced on small knees, while whispered fights had been stilled with stern looks. Hymnbooks and Bibles in hand, the clock was interrupted.

'Does anyone have a hymn we could begin with?'

When the circle in the house on the hill in the middle of everywhere eventually dispersed to their various houses to have their traditional Sunday lunches, the family who lived in this house on the hill went to have their own lunch. The mother set about making dinner for her family of five, and the father, aforementioned interrupter of clocks, went to sit down and enjoy his one day off.

Adrian, twelve, and Ella, eleven, offspring of the pair, were set to peeling, while the youngest, Justin, five, was put in charge of the Table Setting. Table Setter was his favourite job, and the only job he would do without creating what could sometimes be interpreted as the start of World War III by the innocent onlooker. It was just another Sunday, in that house, on the hill, in the middle of everywhere.

Once the meal had been enjoyed, and the dessert had been served and somehow squished into those crevices that dessert always seems to be able to find (even when all others may think the task impossible), the family of five settled into their chairs for the post meal slump.

The parents, Anna and Peter, were discussing the meeting attendees.

'Shame that Alex couldn't join us this morning.'

'Yes, it is really such a shame he has been so sick recently. I hope he'll be able to come out next week.'

'I do hope so. John and Janice's children have become a lot better behaved, though! I'm really noticing a difference in them.'

'Yeah, I think they took my advice to heart.'

'Well, it worked for our three, didn't it? Hasn't harmed you kids yet, has it?'

Ella, Adrian, and Justin glanced at one another and shook their heads, returning to their board game. As the afternoon wore on, they filled the time with their usual Sunday afternoon activities. Games were played, arguments had, and the mandatory walk was performed after a lot of discussion between the kids and Anna about how healthy it really was for them. For Ella, the time seemed to pass quickly, and yet very slowly, as it often did on days like these – days with a big decision to be made.

All too soon, it was time for Ella to get ready to make the most important step of her life. Heart hammering in her chest, she pulled back on the clothes that she had worn in the meeting. She admired herself in the mirror, and then remembered to criticise herself for thinking too positively about her natural assets. They had heard in the meeting that morning that God loved the modest the most after all. She brushed her hair carefully and pulled it back into a bun, a skill she had learned last year for occasions just like these. She wrapped her long curly hair around the ponytail, then stuck the pins in one by one, trying to secure it, but inevitably strands escaped, giving her the 'messy bun' look. Her arms were starting to ache, so she forced herself to think about what was ahead. Ella had prayed about this day for nearly a year now, so she knew for certain that this was the right decision.

She shook her head a couple of times check to make sure it was as stable as it appeared to be. She pulled out a hand mirror and checked the back. Her brown curly hair reached the top of her thighs when pulled straight, but only came down to just under her shoulder blades normally. She very rarely got it cut because women were meant to have long hair. Her mum had told her that the women used to wear hats, but they had then decided that it was okay not to as long as the women had long hair, which Ella appreciated. She thought most hats people wore to church looked weird, and she could never get a hat to sit on top of her hair anyway; it would just bounce right off. She would need one of those strings under her chin to keep it in place.

Ella slipped on her shoes, a pair of small white heels, and her look was complete. There were still fifteen minutes before they would have to leave, so she sat and stared at her open Bible for a while in an attempt to read it, hoping it would prepare her more for the choice ahead. She couldn't concentrate on the words but felt comforted by the weight of the text on her lap. When the time came to leave, she quietly piled into the car between her two brothers, who were particularly rowdy that evening. Sundays did that to them. It was worse on the days when they didn't get dragged on a walk, though. As her dad drove them down the long winding roads that led to the gospel meeting, they were bickering about some insignificant thing, as brothers often do. Ella wished they would stop. After all, this day was the most important day of her life. Deciding to serve God would affect her life after death and that was going to be so much longer than life itself would be. Ella enjoyed wondering about the treasures that she would receive in heaven if she was able to get there.

They pulled up to the community hall two minutes before the mission would start. Irish timekeeping wasn't the most accurate, and it wasn't any different between the friends. They sat in the car in silence for a second or two, then suddenly all piled out of the car as a group. Ella's best friend, Hannah, was walking across to the hall as well, but now that Ella was eleven, she knew that it wasn't acceptable to just dash across to her friend; she had to be dignified about it and it couldn't happen until after the meeting. There wasn't time and it would also be frowned on by the other friends who were walking in. You had to be solemn before the meeting, especially if you were going to make such a big decision – or they wouldn't believe that you meant it. Ella walked in behind her mum, who was wearing a long skirt down to her calves, and her brothers, both in neat suits, the same as her dad, followed behind her. They made their way at a reasonable pace to a free row, about five rows from the front. They never sat right at the front – it was not an advisable position when you had young children, as you never quite knew when they were going to randomly behave like children. Best not to have them under the direct gaze of the elderly gentleman and middle-aged man who ran the meeting – the workers.

This meeting wasn't going to be a normal one, Ella knew. Every half year, at the end of the calendar year and just before the summertime, the workers would change the format of the meeting. The normal gospel meeting was: the aforementioned workers would give out a hymn, which everyone would sing, and then the workers would pray. Then came another hymn, after which the workers would speak for a long time, about half an hour each. This was always about a very important topic that they had spent the whole day and evening before praying about. Ella knew this took a whole day at least because they spent so long in their bedrooms when they were staying at their house.

This meeting, however, would be different.

As they sat in their rows – straight lines of a bigger group made up from the earlier circles of the Sunday morning meetings in the area – there was the same silence. As before, this silence was made up of small noises – shuffling feet, the clearing of a throat, and the scrape of chairs and feet as more people came and sat and adjusted their seats. Two chairs and a microphone on a stand stood waiting at the front of the hall.

After the family had been sat down for only a minute, the old worker made his way to the front of the hall. He moved slowly, shuffling his feet, and sat down in the right-hand chair with a heavy finality. There was no acknowledgement made to any of those sitting there; he just looked into the middle distance for a moment and then opened up his Bible. The other worker followed, sitting on the free chair. He too opened his book, but this time it was his hymnbook, a smaller black book made up of hymns written specifically for the friends. He stood at the front of the hall and welcomed them all.

'Very glad to see you all here today. Could we begin with hymn number thirty-two? Hymn number three-two.'

A keyboard started up, the pianist slowly making their way through the notes in front of them. They played a phrase and started again, this time with all the people in the gathering joining in. Ella always cringed a little when the singing started. Some people liked to choose their own notes, starting and finishing on random ones, leading to a slightly discordant noise to the ear. But the words were always beautiful. God the saviour, the one and only, serving him with a glad noise, even if it wasn't necessarily a tuneful one. Ella could barely concentrate on any of these details today, though. She would normally observe more, noticing new outfits, new relationships, new visitors. She would sometimes even know who was sitting behind her without looking (only the little kids looked around). She could tell just by their voice. But today she didn't know and didn't really care. She was here for a more important reason. When the workers had prayed, they announced that the meeting was going to be open to those with testimonies to share. George, the middle-aged, bald worker, then picked up the microphone off its stand and stood, waiting for people to start standing up, an indication that they had something they wanted to share.

An old lady stood up, one of those whose names Ella could never remember.

'I'm so grateful to still be here today, and that the Lord has kept me within His care for all these years. I would never have found the riches of this way if it hadn't been for a faithful friend. I was going to a worldly church and was very unsatisfied with everything that was happening within the organisation. I had expected more from an organisation that was led by God. I happened to be talking about this at work one day and a co-worker – who I knew to be very upstanding, always very modest with her buns and long skirts – came over to me afterwards and invited me to a gospel meeting. At the start, I was very hesitant as I didn't want to have to wear skirts like that lady always did. But something was drawing me to that meeting, so I went anyway. When I came into the meeting, it was as if the Lord were speaking to me personally. I professed a few months later and I've never been happier. The Lord has a plan for us all; I just hope I can fulfil His desire for my life.' She was crying as she finished.

'Amen,' a few answered.

Others stood up, expressing similar sentiments. Most of them had grown up in the Truth and had never left. Some had left and come back after they had been sent a sign or an experience by God to turn back and re-join the Truth. Some cried, others spoke low, but they were all serious. This was a serious matter, and joy and gladness had to be expressed with crying and seriousness. One particular story stood out to Ella, a story by a woman who had professed when she was only seven years old. She related how God had spoken to her when she was very young and barely understood what she was doing, the choice she was making. Her main point, however, was about how she had never regretted the choice that she had made.

'I have fought with some of the other choices that God wanted me to make, but I have never fought with that first choice, ever since I made it. I long that God would give me the power to keep making that choice, to lay down my life for him and to choose to serve him.'

Ella cried along with the woman. It touched her very deeply. She now knew for certain that God wanted her to make her choice today.

George eventually stood up again and brought the microphone to its resting place at the front of the hall. He gave out another hymn.

'This decision to serve God, it is very important. This is a life-or-death decision. We don't know when the Lord will come, and we don't want to be among those who are found wanting. I will open the meeting now. If anyone wants to make their choice to serve God known tonight, stand up in the chorus after the second, third, or fourth verse.'

Ella's heart started pounding so hard, she was certain everyone could hear it. She felt her knees start to shake a little. The keyboard was hammered out, getting slowly through the introduction, then the first verse, first chorus. Ella took a breath, her first since the hymn had started. She wasn't breathing, and the lack of oxygen meant she was slightly out of breath by the time she remembered to inhale. The second verse started. Ella felt her heart speed up to an all-time fast pace. The second chorus started.

Stand up, she willed herself. *Stand up, nice and easy.* Her body didn't budge. It was like she had taken root in the chair and it wasn't letting go easily. She felt shame wash over her as the second chorus ended and the third verse started. Doubts crept into her head, the devil she knew. The third verse started to end, and as the chorus started, she managed to put her legs down and bear weight on them, standing up. Her eyes were downcast, and she thought about how she had probably never had such a problem with standing up since she had first taken physical steps. She sat down again, keeping her eyes and head concentrated towards the floor. Only when the last chorus was finished was she able to breathe in any way that resembled normality. Her hands were still shaking, though. When Ella glanced up at her mum sitting beside her, she saw tears in her mother's eyes.

On the way out of the meeting, while shaking her hand in the usual line-up on the way out, the worker told her that she would have to read her Bible every day. Ella nodded and smiled, thinking very quietly that that would be hard to remember, but not too loud because she knew that God could see her thoughts. She was afraid thoughts like that would be a disappointment to Him, especially so soon after she'd dedicated her life to him.

Driving home from the meeting, her whole family were commenting on what Ella had done, apart from Justin, who was too young to understand what had happened. Her mum told Ella that the angels in heaven were rejoicing about her making her choice. Her dad spoke about her job to speak in the meeting now and how they would help her with that. Adrian asked her what it had been like. He wasn't professing yet, and Ella told him happily that it had been hard but that it was definitely worth everything. She was floating on a cloud, so happy and at peace with her choice. She wanted to be like those people who had spoken. Some of them had been professing their whole lives, and if she could, she wanted to have such a strong testimony of her faith someday.

Chapter Two

Adrian was unhappy with this new turn of events. His younger sister had decided to serve God and he still wasn't feeling ready to join her. He had never felt any sort of pull to make that kind of a decision; he had always been content not to listen in the meetings. He did realise that he should probably think seriously about it at some point, but he found it so hard to concentrate when the workers and friends were speaking. They went on for ages, speaking in riddles about subjects he just could not seem to wrap his head around. He was now dreading the pressure that would be put on him to choose the same path as his sister.

He was just going with it at the moment, but he could not imagine himself sitting in the meeting every other day for the rest of his life. Boring was the word that sprang to mind when he considered this possibility. He supposed he was lucky; he saw how much Ella had struggled with having to wear a skirt and her hair long in class while the style was short hair and jeans. She had to wear a skirt anyway in school, as that was part of the uniform, but when the non-uniform days came or if she wanted to hang out with her school friends, there was always a crying match. Whereas, when he didn't have to wear the uniform, Adrian just walked into school in his day-to-day clothes without thinking about it too much.

There were benefits, of course; he had met some of his best friends at conventions, a yearly occurrence with big groups of the friends. He had always enjoyed running around, wreaking havoc with them in between meetings, but he knew that that would not last forever. All this thinking about it was making him anxious, though, so he shifted his concentration back to the stupid maths homework Miss Guernsey had set them, groaning as he did. This wasn't much better as an option.

It was Saturday night already, and he had to get all of his homework done before midnight, as they were not allowed to do homework on Sundays, no matter how important it was. His parents didn't listen whenever he told them that that wasn't how the teachers saw it; they just made him live with the consequences. Of course, it didn't help that they had to go to gospel meetings on Tuesdays and Friday nights, in addition to leaving the whole of Sunday work-free. But when asked, his parents would point out that Ella had managed it so far, alongside piano lessons, swimming lessons, and horse-riding lessons. The fact that Ella was two years younger of course wasn't a valid argument according to his mum and dad. When he got too vocal about anything these days, they would just exchange glances and say 'Guess this is what we're in for now' or 'What is he going to be like as a teen' to each other in an irritated way, and if he pushed it too far, he'd get a taste of whatever his dad had at hand.

When he had finished his homework at eleven pm and went to go to bed, he glanced over at the Bible and hymnbook. They'd been gifted to him on his seventh birthday, when he'd been deemed old enough to be able to read the Bible if he wanted to. Ella had been given her Bible and hymnbook at six and a half because she had asked for it one day as she sat reading a comic book. Her parents had immediately ordered one for her, delighted at her asking. Ella was always the 'good' child, while Adrian felt like he was constantly disappointing his parents and falling far below their high standards, as though he were attempting the high jump and had crawled under the bar on purpose. He sighed as he ignored the books' presence and climbed into bed, stepping over the discarded clothes on the way. Shaking off his doubts, he tried to sleep. He just couldn't, though, his mind feeling full of doubts and ways in which he was going to disappoint his parents further. At around two am, he had made up his mind. He was going to make his choice, too; he was going to get his parents off his back and hopefully then he would feel some pride in himself.

There was still one more night of the gospel meeting and he knew that he would probably get the chance to do it then. It would be inconvenient, having to stay awake for the meetings and to have something prepared every week, but maybe it would give him this perfect peace they all kept banging on about.

The next morning, Adrian sat in his spot in the circle, eyes wide open, trying to pretend he'd got more than three hours of sleep that night. He had tried coffee for the first time, sneaked some out of the pot while his parents' backs were turned, and his head was now feeling like an angry bee. He was very close to running out of the room and jumping all the way around the house, but then his parents wouldn't believe him later on when he tried to stand up and they would probably know he was just faking it. Instead, he tapped his toes as much as he could inside his shoes. He didn't know that his parents had figured out where the coffee had gone, as their son had spoken very quickly, starting about ten different sentences but never finishing them as they waited for the first person to walk in. His sister had sat quietly looking at her feet. She was clearly terrified. Adrian only heard the clock and the hundreds of thoughts whizzing through his brain as they sat waiting for everyone to arrive.

Adrian never remembered how he managed to sit through that meeting without running out and circling the house, but somehow he didn't. His sister made it through her very quiet, very short message. She spoke on the first hymn, which asked to be taught the story of Jesus.

'I just want to learn more about Jesus and to follow his footsteps closely so he may lead me until the end.'

Quite a profound lesson from an eleven-year-old, her parents agreed afterwards, quietly proud of their daughter and how God had led them to have such an influence on her. All those mornings spent praying with the door open and reading in the sitting room seemed to have helped at least one of their children so far.

Adrian felt the pressure even stronger after his sister had spoken so nicely in the meeting. He was now worrying about how he would create his own image of professing-ness. He would never forget that first message of hers, but his memory of the moment would change over time. That was, of course, a long time from now, and his current impression was that she was a true servant of God. He already suspected that she would go in the work.

That Sunday played out similarly to the previous one, but this time his dad had complained to his mum in between times that they didn't have enough visitors over,

so this Sunday his mum was doing all the work and
preparing dinner for people his dad wanted to invite over,
while his dad chatted to the other dad and the other mum
and daughter helped out. There was a boy about Adrian's
age in the family, so they spent the day kicking a football
about and trying to avoid Justin, who couldn't quite kick a
ball in any particular direction or with any particular force
yet, so he would quite frequently just lie down crying when
the older boys yelled at him for not doing it right. Ella
swooped in after about five repeats of the same situation
and persuaded Justin to play pretend school with her.

When they arrived at the gospel meeting that
evening, Adrian was very nervous. He knew he was going
to have to do this tonight or there wouldn't be another
chance for another half year. He wanted to get it out of the
way, so he determinedly stood up on the first chorus of the
hymn that the workers had chosen this week to try and
persuade those not yet persuaded to take the step. The
workers had spoken this evening and had quite
convincingly painted the hell he would go to if he didn't
get his act together, so he figured professing was probably
worth it if his parents were going to get off his back *and* it
would mean not going to hell. He thought of the hell that
had been described by the workers in the same way he
imagined the losers of the battles he had had when he was
younger and incredibly bored, with the same heroes and
villains he had created using the superhero dolls. To
Adrian, the hell was on par with where the villains would
be sent to rot.

Before Adrian got the chance to speak in a meeting,
there were special meetings which had too many people,

and he really didn't want to speak there the first time. Special meetings ran over Christmas this year and that meant that they spent their Christmas Day at a special meeting, which consisted mainly of trying to listen for two two-hour slots as a group of workers spoke. The friends occasionally got a chance to stand up and speak, which Adrian found slightly more interesting, as it broke the hours up slightly. In between the meeting, there was lunch where everyone had sandwiches in their cars. Some people branched out and ate their sandwiches in someone else's car, while some ate their sandwiches in the hall itself. At least it didn't last the whole day, so his parents were able to tell Ella and Justin, who were both waiting for presents from Santa, that Santa had waited until they would have more time to fully enjoy the presents.

A week later, Adrian sat once again in the circle, on four hours' sleep this time (but without the coffee because it wasn't worth it). He spoke of Jesus and how He had told His followers to forgive all sins against them, no matter how often they had sinned. He had considered that his parents should hear this message as they became very annoyed when he accidentally dropped dishes and he had done that quite frequently the last week, dropping a total of five cups and two plates, leading his mother to suspect he was doing it on purpose.

Afterwards, everyone told both him and Ella that they had done very well, and Adrian finally felt a bit more settled about the whole thing, similar to when his results came out and it turned out that he had passed the year after all. So, he got on with things and spoke in every meeting, managing somehow to come up with important messages and keeping his parents happy. He would forget to pray and read the Bible with a predictable regularity and feel a guilt about this every time this happened, but he pushed that down. He had more important things on which to concentrate.

Chapter Three

Anna sat watching the sun go down, her husband kneeling on the bed behind her. She was thinking back to when she had professed – her children's professing had made her think more about that day. She had been brought up in the Truth, just like her kids had, as had both of her parents and their parents before them. She was third generation. Unfortunately, neither of her parents were now professing; only her three brothers and herself had continued. She knew why they had stopped professing, and some part of her felt sorry for her parents, but she also knew that God didn't make mistakes and that those workers had been working through God when they had kicked her parents out. 'God doesn't like you questioning His works,' she had overheard them telling her parents.

She had been sitting in her room, just above the room where they were talking, so she had heard a lot more of the conversation than her parents knew. Since that conversation, her parents had stopped going to meetings. It hadn't stopped sixteen-year-old Anna and her older brothers from going. Her parents had tried to persuade them that the workers were lying about what they had said, but the workers had already told Anna and her brothers the truth of the matter – that her parents were losing their faith and that they would try to persuade the four of them to go down with them. When her parents had done exactly what the worker said they would do, they knew that they were right in their ways, so they were able to hold strong until they eventually all left home one by one and got married.

Anna had already professed at fourteen, having spent many sleepless nights worrying about how she would go to hell if she didn't. She still remembered the perfect peace that had come with finally submitting herself to God's will. When she met Peter and got past the fact that he had dated someone outside of the church, they got married at the tender ages of twenty-one and twenty-two after dating for a year and a half. Now they had three kids of their own, and while the kids had met their grandparents and had spent Christmas together, they didn't really know them all that well. Anna had never really forgiven her parents for leaving the meetings, and now didn't recognise her mother in the lady who wore jeans occasionally and even used the Lord's name in vain sometimes. Not in front of her, but she'd heard her mother say it under her breath in another room. Anna missed the mother whom she had grown up with – a quiet, humble woman who wore long skirts with her hair in a bun and who always submitted to her husband. Her dad had not changed much; he looked and sounded the same to her, but the changes in Anna's mother, Anna found irreconcilable.

Anna prayed every night and morning for her parents' return to the meetings. She prayed that they would be forgiven and that they would be able to bring themselves to come back, that God would reveal what was most important to them. Now that her own children were professing, she felt the need to pray even harder for her parents' return to the fold.

When her husband had said his prayers, she joined him in bed and fell asleep, her head still full with thoughts of her parents. She had said her prayers and read her Bible before he came up to bed. The next day, her mother messaged her, asking how everyone was, as she did every month. Anna answered quickly. Normally she had to take time to prepare herself, to ensure that she would be in the right spirit to allow God to answer through her. This time, however, she had big news to share with her. She told her mum that Adrian and Ella had professed and her mum immediately called her. 'Hey, Anna, I'm sure you must be delighted!'

'I really am, it's such a wonderful step that they have both taken.' Anna felt a little bit sorry for her mother sometimes, knowing she was missing out on so many wonderful things by not going to the meetings, but she believed that God would reveal the light to her mother someday and she would come back.

'Yeah, I'm glad you're happy for them,' her mother said gently.

'How are you both anyway?'

'We're both well, thank you. We were wondering if we could come and visit the kids at some point? We both really miss them, and we really miss you both, too.'

Anna sighed. Every time her mother called, it was the same story. They wanted to visit. As a mother, she could understand her mum's perspective, of course, but between the meeting and the gatherings and looking after the kids, she had little time to fit her mum in.

'We're very busy at the moment, Mum. Maybe we can meet another time. I have to go now – the kids are

coming downstairs and I need to get them their breakfast.'
She said goodbye and hung up, feeling a little uneasy – as
she did every time she spoke to her mum. But Anna shook
it off and began preparing breakfast.

Chapter Four

Six years later

Ella couldn't sit still. They were in the car on the way to convention, and she was buzzing to see all her friends again. Convention was her favourite time of the year and this year she had an important decision to make. Justin and Adrian sat on both sides of her, playing the DS they had eventually persuaded their parents to buy. Peter and Anna had only agreed because another family near them had also bought one for their kids, and they were some of the more upstanding friends in the area. Adrian was engaged in an intense Mario Kart race with Justin, and Justin was twisting and turning as if that would make his car turn faster. They let out the occasional giggles and screams, both of them fully invested in the game. Ella was trying to read her book, but she couldn't concentrate. This convention was two hours away from where they lived, otherwise they would be expected to sit quietly, to prepare for the spirit of the convention, but their parents knew their kids and didn't expect them to sit and do nothing for two hours. Adrian was able to drive himself now, but his car had broken down recently and was getting repairs at the workshop.

When they arrived at the convention, the boys had fallen out several times over various races that Adrian had won. Adrian had never believed in the philosophy of letting his younger brother win just because of his age, even occasionally. He figured that Justin wouldn't go easy on him when they were both grown up anyway. They stepped out of the car in a jumble of slightly sticky bodies, a result of the unusual twenty-five-degree Celsius weather combined with the car's broken air conditioner. They stretched out the cramps and breathed in the fresh air, looking around the familiar setting. The tent was standing there as it always had been. People walked around, speaking in hushed tones to those they hadn't seen in a year. Everyone always smiled and greeted one another, even if they didn't have time to stop and chat.

The family had pulled up beside the girls' sleeping quarters, as Ella and her mum had packed their things in last. Ella and Anna hastily grabbed their bags, sleeping bags, and pillows, in an annual attempt to carry all of their items in one go. As was also an annual tradition, they dropped the bags halfway to the sleeping quarters. Thankfully this year the weather had been good in the run up, so the bags didn't get covered in mud like they had the last couple of years. They resigned themselves to two trips and went with the sleeping bags and pillows quickly into their pre-booked beds, as they had messaged the lead sister worker of the grounds four weeks ago to book them. They found them in the right places, Ella in between her two best friends, and Anna beside her friends. Neither had seen their friends yet. One of Ella's friends, Grace, lived on the convention grounds, but still came out to join her and Hannah for the company every year since she was seven. Her doing this also meant that her room was free for the older workers who needed to stay somewhere warmer than the old metal army huts most of the workers stayed in.

They went back out to grab the rest of the luggage and set them in their places, rolling out the sleeping bags on the creaky, slightly unstable-looking metal bedframes with thin mattresses.

Last year, Anna had brought Ella and Adrian down here to the convention and left them for the week just before the convention had started. Ella had slept on a spare bed in Grace's room, while her brother stayed in with the brother workers. They had been there other times during preps (preparing the area for the convention), when some of their jobs had been wiping down the old bedframes and hanging the curtains to divide the large shed into slightly smaller segments. Ella had also helped with washing all of the dishes and packing them into boxes ready for the convention, so they knew that all of the dishes had been washed at least once. They of course had had to do that job on the hottest day of the year, and although plenty of ice lollies had been provided, it was still thoroughly unpleasant as they used boiling hot water that steamed the wash-up shed like a sauna. It was good for their pores, they had joked.

The men had done very different jobs, washing down sheds, hanging up lights, setting up mics, putting the seats in their places, while the women went around cleaning everything, seemingly the only job the women were allowed to do – at least that was what Ella was told when she had asked. Cleaning dishes, tables, chairs, beds, walls. As someone with two brothers, Ella had always found this a bit unfair. She was just as good as Adrian at drilling holes in things and she found the jobs she was given often slightly mindless and boring, but she knew that it was all for the big picture. After all, she had enjoyed a sense of achievement when everyone arrived, knowing that she had helped with the process. No one had noticed, though, but she knew that was also important; the things she did without recognition would be recognised in eternity – that's what the workers often said.

Adrian was not looking forward to coming to the convention, for the same reason that he had become a quieter person. He was slowly disliking the meetings more and more, and had regular fights with his parents about going to the gospel meeting, telling them he was too busy at school and too tired most nights. His parents had had regular talks with him, warning him about straying too close to the edge. They had quoted one of the workers in the field's regular stories about how he had gone to missions even though he had been busy in college and the reward he had got from doing this. His mother had got upset, his father angry, both of them asking him why, but Adrian couldn't bring himself to tell them the real reason. The quiet dread had turned to terror as they had drawn closer to their destination. His breathing became more and more shallow, and his stomach was starting to hurt.

Ella was completely unaware of how her brother was feeling and was happily anticipating the arrival of her friends as she helped her mother to bring the necessary home-baked goods down to the cookhouse. There was a tradition to make something to bring with you to convention. You had to remember to only be positive about anything anyone made, though. Just in case the person who

had made them was standing beside you, embarrassed. Ella
had learnt that lesson the hard way.

In the cookhouse, where all the meals were made,
Ella found Grace and Hannah. They hugged and caught up
with one another as Ella fell in beside them, drying the
dishes. There were workers on either side of them; one of
them was a worker returned from labouring in Norway.
Another man walked up as they were halfway through.

'Can I join you guys?'

'Yeah of course!' Hannah handed him the tea towel
she had been using. 'Thanks for doing my job!' She started
walking away but turned back around. 'Just kidding!' She
pulled a face and grabbed another tea towel.

'I'm going to have to start working twice as fast
now,' Grace teased but she got to it immediately.

The man introduced himself as Gareth.

'Where is your accent from, Gareth?

'Canada. I'm just visiting Ireland for a short time,
then I'll be moving on to the other European conventions.'

They nodded. Workers quite often did a Europe
route, going from one convention to the next.

'So what field were you in last?'

'I was in Saskatchewan, in the city Saskatoon.'
They nodded.

'Yeah, totally,' Ella said, then added, 'Where is
that?'

He laughed. 'It's kinda in the middle, like, have you
heard of Vancouver?'

They had.

'Yeah, so it's two provinces over.' He smiled
broadly.

'Oh, so you might know Jane and Peter? They moved to Vancouver last year.'

'Well, Vancouver is a sixteen-hour drive away, so I don't, but if I'm ever there for convention, I'll keep an eye out for 'em.'

'Oh wow. You can't drive sixteen hours to get to anywhere here,' Ella said.

'Just the sea,' Hannah said. 'But then your car will be wet.'

'Yeah, Canada is kinda big, I've been told.' He winked.

'Are there many in your field?' Hannah wanted to know.

'Yeah, there are quite a few, and we've had a bit of interest. There is this couple, they just lost their son in a tragic accident.' The girls all expressed their sympathies. 'Yeah, it was awful, but they have been showing some interest in the meetings recently. So, who knows, God puts us through experiences for a reason.'

'Yeah, maybe that was the sign that they were needing to find the way. Have they been coming out long?'

'About a year. We first came across them when we were knocking on doors, handing out the cards.'

'Huh, we just put the cards through the letterboxes – maybe we should be chatting to people, too.'

They chatted for a while, and after the dishes were finished, they parted from Graham. There was a feeling just before convention that felt full of nostalgia for Ella, of memories both made and those yet to be made. There was a constant hush, the waiting for the crowds to come the next day, mixed with greetings by close friends and kids who were running around with new and old friends. As they washed and dried the last of the dishes, there was already a feeling of the convention going too quickly that made her want to slow down the moments into individual future memories.

Adrian was sitting in the bathroom stall, shaking. He had seen him again. He didn't know how he could cope with the next few days. He felt like every single moment was dragging. It couldn't go quickly enough for him. He felt overwhelmed with a guilt that part of him knew wasn't rational, but he couldn't push it away even with this knowledge. He sat with his face in his hands and felt tears starting their way down his face, dripping through his fingers. Great. Now he knew he was truly weak. Tears were the last thing he needed. He took a shaky, slow deep breath in and out, and hoped his heart wasn't actually audible outside his own ears. His dad's voice came to him. *'Are you a girl, Adrian? Why are you getting so emotional then? Real men don't cry. If you don't stop, I'll give you a reason to cry.'* He knew it wasn't strictly fair as he had seen various men cry, but he had never forgotten the sentiment. Weakness was attached to crying. It was a vulnerability.

When Adrian had taken a few more shaky breaths, he stepped out and checked himself in one of the few mirrors hanging on the wall. It thankfully wasn't obvious that he had been crying. He sent a quick prayer to the God who had let this happen that He would help him get through at least this meal. After all, God never gives more than you can handle, right? He hoped it was true.

Ella helped serve the food. For most of convention, this was the men's job, but for the night before convention started, the women still served the food. Afterwards, it became too big a job for mere women. She tugged slightly at the hem of her skirt. It was a denim skirt, just simple, practical for helping out, but she had seen a couple of sister workers glance at her, and she felt self-conscious about its length, which was just above the knee. She was scooping out portions of rice when she saw Adrian. He looked a bit dour, scowling at everything.

'Adrian, scrape that expression off your face or everyone is going to think that you don't want to be here.' Ella half-laughed at the idea.

Adrian smiled, but it didn't quite reach his eyes. She decided she was going to have to pray a bit harder for her brother, otherwise he might miss out. At least he was at convention, though, the best place to be when you're on the fence. She hoped he wouldn't get stuck in the hedge, like sheep they heard about in the meetings that were trying to escape often did.

Adrian had never really prescribed to everything the way Ella did. Ella always believed every word the workers said, while Adrian naturally questioned everything that he was told. Once, when being told off by his parents for questioning too much about the meetings and being called a petulant child by his father, Adrian had argued that they were often told to be more childlike, or was that only for the childlike tendencies that meant that the workers could get away with saying anything? That had resulted in a long

lecture about how the workers gave up so much to bring
the gospel message, that the message was sent directly
from God, and how dare he question things that the
workers said. Adrian still privately thought the workers
mustn't have ever met a child before to say such things
about them. Kids were annoying and could be very full of
themselves – in Adrian's experience, once they passed the
new-born stage, they mostly weren't the meek and gentle
beings the workers spoke of. Although, how could workers
really know? They mostly stayed with families for short
periods of time, and the kids were generally prepared to be
on their best behaviour while the workers were around.
Adrian remembered being brought out of the room anytime
he started to misbehave when the workers were staying in
the house. He shivered as he thought of that fateful day he
had forgotten about for so many years when that worker
had stayed in their house.

Adrian shook his thoughts off and went to sit down
beside his best friend, Harry. Harry had black hair and was
gay. The latter was a big secret that Adrian had kept ever
since Harry had told him one midnight outside the sleeping
quarters. They were sitting on a bench when Harry had
turned to him.

'Adrian, can you keep a big secret?' Harry
whispered. He had been very quiet all evening, so Adrian
had suspected that something was up.

'Yeah sure, what's up?'

'I think I might be gay.'

Adrian had stayed very still, trying to proccss what
he had just been told.

'I think it may mean that God doesn't love me like he loves others …' Harry began to sob silently. 'But I don't know what to do about it, I didn't know who else to tell. Sorry to burden you with this secret, but it's just … it's too much. I don't think I can ever find love. I don't know how I can cope with that, never being able to love someone openly.'

Adrian had put his arm around his friend.

'But you always admired girls with me?'

'Yeah, I wanted to be straight, and to be fair, I can still see when girls are pretty. I'm gay, not blind.'

'Harry, of course God still loves you. It is unfortunately a battle you're going to live with for the rest of your life, but God never gives us more than we can handle.'

'I think it's more than I can handle,' Harry had said in a small voice.

Adrian nodded. 'It is one of the harder battles to fight, but pray about it.'

Harry didn't know that Adrian was going through anything now, but Adrian knew he would probably tell his friend because he knew he could trust him. They had been friends for a long time.

He greeted Harry and they compared their opinions on the recent soccer match. It was their shared passion, and it didn't take long for them to be in a heated debate over whether the goalie was purposefully being an idiot that year or not. Anna, sitting beside Harry, poked Adrian and Harry and told them to be quiet, as their discussion had started to become quite loud.

Adrian was glad to forget his worries for a while and settled into a slightly calmer conversation with Harry.

'What did you bring this year for snacks?'

'I have a few packets of sweets, three tins of Pringles and a few packets of pot noodle – I think twelve should be enough to carry us through?'

Adrian laughed.

'I hope it will be. Otherwise, we'll be going hungry, and we can't have that now, can we?'

'No, that wouldn't do at all.' Harry's eyes flicked to Adrian's.

Adrian felt a sudden jolt in his stomach that he pushed down as he always had. He liked girls, he knew he did, but being in Harry's presence reminded him of when he had kissed that girl Julie for the first time. There was a sudden excitement to it. He cleared his throat and forced himself to think about other things.

When Ella was finished giving food to everyone who had arrived, she sat down between Hannah and Grace and started eating her own meal.

'How was preps?' Ella asked Grace, before taking her first bite of the sweet-and-sour pork with rice. It tasted good after a long day.

'Yeah, great! We were a little short of male help, but it all came together in the end as it always does.'

'No, I'm okay, thanks.'

They turned around at the sound of a deep voice none of the three recognised. It was a boy of about their age with beautiful curly dark hair, dark eyes, and a cute face. He was also tall, a bonus for the five-foot-seven Ella.

Her heart fluttered in a way she had never experienced
before, and all thought of eating went straight out of her
head. She realised she was staring about thirty seconds
later when she got poked either side in the ribs by her best
friends.

'Ow!'

'You're staring!'

'Ooooh, who's got a little crush?' Their eyes were
dancing.

'He is *cute*,' she whispered to them, still thinking of
his beautiful hair. She wanted to know who that cutie was.
He was exactly her type, but she knew she was not pretty
enough to be an option for him to go for with her frizzy
brown hair, glasses, and braces. She also knew her
personality was too awkward, and that she dressed like a
thirty-year-old nun if the bullies at school were to be
believed. They seemed to make a lot of comments about
Ella, and they had had quite a few points to make about all
the different rules that Ella needed to follow in the Truth.
The fact that Ella didn't own a TV and had very little
general exposure to popular culture made the other kids at
school laugh, which Ella didn't understand on any level.
She also discovered she was very innocent because most of
the jokes the bullies made about boys' and girls' relations
went straight over her head. So, all in all, Ella knew she
wasn't a catch. The bullies had made sure her knowledge
was up to date in that regard, even if they didn't enlighten
her on the other subjects.

But Ella knew that she had the upper hand on some
level, she knew she was going to go to heaven if she
managed to stay in the Truth and listen to the workers, read

and pray, and follow the rules every day for the rest of her life. She was quite looking forward to dying actually, an odd wish for a seventeen-year-old perhaps, but if you know your life afterwards will be much better, why wouldn't you enjoy the thought of being numbered among the few? The bullies wouldn't make it to heaven because they weren't professing, not that Ella didn't hope they would see the light in her, repent, apologise, and then start professing. Ella dreamed of that day to distract from the reality of school sometimes.

Now, though, they ate quickly, Ella still thinking of the cute boy behind her, almost imagining she could feel his presence behind her. Even though she knew she didn't have a chance with him, there was no harm in dreaming about him, was there? Grace had a crush on a boy as well, a boy from school, which wasn't really allowed, but she said she wasn't going to act on it, and it was just a crush, so Ella figured that that was okay. They were pretty sure this other slightly creepy boy, George, had a crush on Grace, but she didn't like him back. He did slightly strange things, like leaving notes on her seat last year. He had left one for every meeting and it had only served to creep Grace and her friends out, something they had all been quite vocal about when they saw him. Ella suspected he wouldn't be put off by this.

Hannah didn't seem to have a crush on anyone at the moment, but she did appreciate what she called a 'fine specimen,' and Ella suspected unknown boy number one would fall into said 'fine specimen' category. But that discussion would happen later, and in the present Grace got up and went to help with the seemingly never-ending flow of dishes as she hadn't helped with serving the food.

Ella jumped when someone sat down in the empty spot beside her.

'Can I sit here?'

'I think you already are,' she laughed, then realised who she was talking to and instantly turned tomato soup red, she knew, as she felt her cheeks heat up.

'I'll take that as a yes then.' His voice was deep.

'I'm Ella.' She was surprised her voice was in any way understandable.

'Guy.'

'Where are you from, Guy?'

'I'm from Spain – my name is technically Guillermo but people here have a problem with the pronunciation of that word, I've discovered.' He laughed and she joined in. She would have liked to stay and talk to him for longer, but Hannah was also standing up and helping clear tables, so Ella excused herself and helped Hannah out, avoiding eye contact, hoping that Guy would feel that her lack of interest was an attractive quality and that it actually showed her interest in him.

Guy, being a typical male, read it as the opposite, but Ella didn't know this. She kept working and when she looked up the next time, Guy/ Guillermo was gone. Ella felt like she had dreamt him.

Bedtime came too soon, as they had worked until late in the evening, only finishing serving food at nine pm, so they didn't have a lot of time for their daily evening walk before the ten pm lights out curfew. They had to be quiet as they sneaked back in, quietly changing and slipping into their sleeping bags to gather in a huddle and whisper about Guy/Guillermo. When that subject had been exhausted, which took longer than you'd think considering Ella had only exchanged a few words with him, Grace told them of the latest adventures of George.

'So . . . you'll never guess George's last great idea.' Grace began, grinning at the girls, who had their heads close together as they sat cross-legged on the beds they had pulled together.

'What did he do?' Ella pushed her hair back from her face and fixed her pyjama t-shirt.

'Well, you know how much he loves farming, and I suppose he wants a girlfriend who also loves it, so he bought me a sheep.'

'A sheep?' Hannah echoed, looking horrified. Hannah had a deep-rooted fear of sheep since a ram had knocked her over as a kid.

'Yeah, a sheep. One sheep.'

'Aren't they meant to live in groups?'

'Exactly, so he bought me this sheep and had the great idea of bringing it to me and letting it out in the yard to show me.'

'Wouldn't he just put it in a field to show you there?'

'You'd think' Grace giggled and her friends joined in. Grace lived on a farm, but she was the opposite of a farmer. She avoided helping with anything farming related as if her life depended on it. Any time the friends stayed over, Hannah and Ella would be helping fix fences and chase cattle faster than Grace would be.

'So, when George arrive with my new sheep.'
Grace continued, pulling a face at the word sheep, 'He
opened the back of the trailer to show me my new present.'
At this, Grace started laughing uncontrollably.

'He had forgotten though, to stand in front of the
sheep, and my brand-new sheep skipped out of there and
past poor George, who hadn't seen the great Houdini make
a run for it.' Hannah and Ella were joining in the hysterics.

'Well, the sheep decides to give mum's brand-new
plants a taste, and destroys them, which essentially ends up
in mum chasing George as George chased the sheep. It was
so funny, and it lasted ridiculously long.' The girls were
rolling on the bed now, laughing uncontrollably. The idea
of Grace's neat and dignified mother chasing a lad and his
sheep was hilarious to them. Their mirth was apparently a
bit too loud, though, and they received some *shh*'s from
some older ladies in the corner, who were reading their
bibles.

Duly chastened, the girls set to reading their own
Bibles and saying their prayers. During the year, Ella
always found it hard to read and pray in a meaningful way,
unless something unusual, scary, or exciting was
happening, but she could always read and pray in a true
way at convention. Convention gave her a new focus to
truly serve God in a way she struggled to do the rest of the
year. When she had opened her heart to God and felt fully
at peace and connected to him, she read a few verses she
had been considering speaking on in the meeting when she
got a chance. Convention was an important time to tell
your testimony, especially when you were getting baptised.
Fully settled to sleep, Ella turned onto her back and drifted

off to sleep, dreaming of Guys and Guillermo's who liked
her back.

Chapter Five

Ella woke up to the sound of an alarm clock. She opened her eyes slowly, disorientated. As the alarm clock continued its cry, she glanced at her own and groaned. People waking up at five am to get an early hot shower were pretty annoying. This was always made worse when they didn't immediately wake up to the sound of their alarm clock and instantly turn it off. There was a clatter as the alarm clock, still ringing, fell under the bed. At least Ella presumed this is what happened, as her eyes wouldn't open enough to really figure out what was going on. After a bit of a scuffle and a few more groans, the alarm clock was located and switched off.

Ella turned over and tried to go back to sleep, but with the ringing of the alarm clock, her excitement and frustration had been growing. She stayed in bed, slowly waking up until she was fully awake. When she heard the early bird coming back, she decided to take a shower herself. After all, she was already awake and might as well do something with her time. Slowly dragging herself up out of the warmth and comfort of her sleeping bag, she groaned softly, shivering as the cold air touched her skin.

Nope, that's not it, she thought, shuffling back into her sleeping bag until she realised she needed to pee. Reluctantly reaching out of the warmth, she grabbed a hoodie and pulled it into the sleeping bag so it could warm up. Once she was satisfied, she put it on, got up, and quietly gathered the bits she needed. Ella decided against getting dressed for the meeting yet, as she knew she would be helping out at breakfast and her good Saturday outfit would be ruined.

The glances of the sister workers yesterday still in her head, she chose a longer denim skirt, a loose T-shirt, and a pair of flip flops for convenience. She walked out in her pyjamas with the hoodie on top, carrying everything she needed. The sleeping quarters for the women were enclosed in a private space, far away from the male gaze, so she knew she was safe walking around in her pyjamas. The showers were not of the best quality, although they had improved from her childhood when they had had freezing cold and scalding hot showers in equal measure. The water seemed to never be able to decide which temperature it wished to inflict on the innocent, switching between the two with an unpredictable irregularity. It also hadn't mattered which temperature they set the shower to; it just gave out one temperature – suffering. Now they at least could choose if they wanted scalding hot or freezing cold. Ella wasn't sure if she liked it, but she still needed to have a shower, so she went with hot with the occasional touch of freezing cold.

Fully awake, she pulled on her very modest clothes and tried to warm up in the sun before she went back into the shed, as the hot had run just before she had finished washing off the last of the conditioner. She put her things on her bed in the shed, read, said her prayers and decided to go for a walk – she knew herself and if she didn't go for a walk, she'd end up lying around the shed. Sleep was now impossible. And using her hair dryer, the next step in her plan for the morning, would inevitably end up in her having to sleep outside tomorrow. If people didn't appreciate pre seven am alarms, they abhorred pre seven am hair dryers.

Ella enjoyed the sound of the birds and the sun on her skin. Halfway through the walk, she came across Graham. He smiled at her but didn't say anything. She enjoyed the feeling of the sun and walked slowly back, thinking of what the day would bring. There was a true feeling of peace in her heart, and she was fully ready to hear the messages God would have for her.

After her walk, she made her way back to the sleeping quarters, quietly checking to see that her friends were both still sleeping. She was aware of a few electrical sockets in a hut without any people in it, so she quickly dried her hair. If she didn't dry her hair properly, it would be a frizzy mess for the rest of the day. When she was finished, it was only seven am and breakfast wasn't until eight. She went up to the cookhouse, and helped put bread, milk, and butter out on the tables, something that couldn't happen until the morning of the breakfast. The rest had been set out the night before.

The workers sat at their own separate tables, and these had to be set differently. While the friends only got porridge or cereal, the workers got the extra option of having a fry-up. Normally the workers just sat at a different table, but at this convention, the workers sat behind a wall at the top of the shed, which was on a slope.

Adrian was woken up in a completely different manner.

'Get up get up get up get upgetupupupupupup' It was his youngest cousin, inexplicably headbutting his feet.

He started to climb onto Adrian's bed, going for the jumping method. Adrian rapidly moved his feet up the bed and sat up. While well meaning, this method hurt.

'Okay, Slimy, I'm getting up.' His cousin's name was Simon, but this nickname annoyed Simon and Adrian wasn't a big fan of him at this moment in time.

'Dooonnn'ttt!'

'Well don't wake me and everyone else up like this!' Adrian suddenly realised that there was actually no one else here to wake up. Even Harry was gone. Harry didn't usually eat breakfast, so this was confusing. 'Wait, what time is it, Slimy?'

'Time you were up.' Adrian's uncle and dad were standing in the doorway, his uncle laughing. He would have been the one to send the three-year-old terror in, of course. His dad, however, was not laughing.

'Why are you still in bed? We're halfway through breakfast. If you stay in bed any longer, you'll have to go hungry until ten o'clock tea.' Peters arms crossed over his chest as he spoke.

Adrian wouldn't have really minded sleeping for an extra hour or so, but it didn't seem like he had a choice in the matter. He was also too groggy to argue the point, so he got up, dragged on some clothes, and stomped out of the shed. He was still asleep, which was an observation his uncle and cousin didn't hesitate to make. Like father, like son, Adrian supposed.

Ella saw Adrian slouching in and sliding down a bench further down the shed. She rolled her eyes. This was typical of him. He never showed any enthusiasm for these things and never got up on time in the morning. Normally she didn't pass many remarks on this, but he had really changed this past year and not in any good ways. She turned back to Grace and Hannah.

'I see Graham is speaking last in the first meeting.' The list for the meetings had come out that morning.

'Yeah! That'll be lovely,' said Grace. They discussed this subject for a few more minutes when people started leaving their tables so they had to get up and help clear their tables and reset them for dinner. Ella felt extra helpful when she was one of the last people to leave after setting up the tables.

It was half nine when they were finally finished helping to set up the dining shed for dinner. They went back to the sleeping quarters and changed quickly into their meeting clothes. Ella was wearing a floor-length, navy floral dress with a V-neckline, which she accompanied with a T-shirt underneath. Her mother had told her she had to wear one. The reason behind this, Ella supposed, was that she couldn't wear anything that might possibly show some cleavage. But her mother wasn't so vulgar as to actually say that. She also had a calf-length slip underneath as the dress was see-through in very bright sunlight. It was a floaty garment with the potential to fly up in the wind, so the slip also added a feeling of security. Anna was quite the stickler for ensuring that the friends stayed good, modest girls, and had been known to bring the young girl friends more modest skirts, tops, or a slip, even if she didn't know them personally. Ella supposed this was generous of her mother, but she felt a bit embarrassed when Anna did it.

Guy/Guillermo hadn't been at breakfast earlier. Ella wondered where he was. Maybe he'd stayed at a B&B

nearby. Attempting to shape her bun into something that was passable, Ella sighed. It was so hard putting your hair in a bun with such curly hair. She strongly disliked her hair and wished her mother would let her straighten it. After a few attempts, she dragged the mass into a ponytail. She half-considered leaving it like that – convention wasn't meant to be about your looks anyway, but she remembered her friend's talents.

'Grace?'

'Yes, my dear?'

'Could you save this catastrophe?'

Grace nodded and set to work. She twisted small pieces of hair, using the pins Ella passed back to her while sitting on her bed cross-legged, into an intricate bun that they liked to call 'the Grace special'. When Grace was finished, Ella hugged her friend.

'Thanks for saving me from disaster.'

Grace laughed. 'Anytime. Want to give me Dutch braids?'

Ella did. She plaited two small Dutch braids, which Grace slipped into and around her own simple donut bun. Hannah had her hair in a protective style at the moment, in weaves. It had been a learning process for Ella and Grace as they had tried to learn more about their friend's culture, but they had both discovered a lot through trial and error.

Hannah had experienced racism from some older friends in the area. She had become friends with Grace and Ella when they'd stood up for her at a young age, when Hannah's parents hadn't long in the country. But it was a learning process for the two who had been brought up in privileged white homes, something they both acknowledged and tried to work on regularly.

As a ritual, the girls all complained about hair every time they had to do it at convention and really any time they did it together, but they all secretly loved the process, especially at convention. They sprayed themselves with hairspray, their favourite perfumes, slipped on their highest heels, and went out. They walked to the tent, arms laden with their Bibles, hymnbooks, notebooks, pens, and more than enough sweets to stock a start-up sweetshop.

They went over to the meeting tent to find their seats. They were sitting two rows behind the brother workers. The meeting tent was set out in a very particular fashion, with rows of seats fanned in a semicircle around the centre platform. Rugs and cushions were placed on a handful of seats. There were labels on most of the seats, having been booked weeks ago. The workers' seats were either side of the platform, looking at the side profile of whoever was speaking. The sister workers sat on the left side of the platform and the brothers on the right. The red platform in the middle held two seats either side of a microphone on a stand. The platform raised the person speaking a little, with a curtain hung behind it to make it stand out from the rest of the white tent. Only brother workers ever sat on the platform, as the brother workers had a natural authority over the sister workers. That was how Paul had left it.

They went out into the yard, where people who had been arriving were gathered, getting tea, coffee and various traybakes (anything that can be baked/made in a tray, and sometimes things that can't, like bought biscuits). The three friends were split up by the crowd. They nodded at various family members and people they knew well as they made their way through the throng. People they vaguely recognised but couldn't tell you the name of and people they had never met before also greeted them. Some made light conversation as they all made their way to the end of the line. It took a lot longer to make your way across the yard when everyone else was in the way, standing in groups and wanting to chat to you.

Ella spotted Guillermo and her heart quickened a little. She got her tea, joking with the woman who was pouring it, the lady who played the keyboard in the missions. Her next step was to try and strategically place herself close enough to Guy so he could see her, but she didn't look at him. She hoped he would notice her, or maybe the perfume she'd put on at least. It seemed to work, as he came over to her and her grandmother as they were talking (her dad's mum, her mum's mum hadn't been at a meeting in Ella's living memory).

'Ella, right?'

'Guy! I didn't see you there.' This was a lie, but a necessary one in Ella's eyes. She would try to do better in the coming days.

'How are you doing?'

'Good thanks! Have you met many people?' Grandma Poppy excused herself, winking at Ella discreetly. Ella blushed. She'd hear all about that moment later. She only had to breathe in the vague direction of a boy her age for her grandparents to plan out the wedding. They probably also had the invitations ready and had decided their number of children. They did that sometimes.

Weirdly, that number changed depending on whom they were matching her with. Ella wondered vaguely how many it would be with Guillermo.

They spoke for a few more moments before the crowd started heading towards the meeting tent. They went their separate ways and Ella missed him immediately. But she went into the meeting anyway, sitting beside Grace. Hannah was on the other side of Grace, and she leaned over to whisper.

'Saw you chatting up our Spaniard, romance is brewing!' Giggling, she sat back before Ella could protest.

Ella gathered herself into meeting mood. It was ten minutes before the meeting would start. She glanced down at the list.

Farrow 2011

Saturday

10:30–12:30	2:30–4:30	6:00–7:30
Graham Gilt	Harry Froth	Ashford Peters
David O'Hare	George Walters	William McGurney
Amy Currey	Grace Andrews	
	Katie Hugh	

Sunday

Fred Angel	Thomas Wurst	Timothy Farmer
Sara Wilson	Marjorie Magowan	Beverly Ham
Janneke Dijkstra	Sally Smith	
	Dana McTavish	

Monday

Ashford Peters	Graham Gilt	William McGurney
Aggie Dime	Stan Fields	David O'Hare
Danny Pearl	Katie Hugh	
	Grace Andrews	

Tuesday

10:00–12:00	1:30–3:30
Thomas Wurst	Gareth Gilt
Sally Smith	Fred Angel
Beverly Ham	Marjorie Magowan
	Janneke Dijkstra

Lovely, Ella thought, and settled herself into the meeting.

Chapter Six

Adrian had spent his morning multitasking, both trying to wake up and trying not to have a panic attack. Having seen the speakers list, he now knew he was going to have to listen to the man twice. Because of this, Adrian stayed in the sleeping quarters as long as he could. In an attempt to distract himself, he played 'cut the rope' on his mobile phone. He had barely talked to Harry since last night and was starting to sense that Harry was both worried and annoyed at him. At some point, he was realising, he would have to tell his best friend what was going on with him. He really didn't want to have to talk about it, though. At two minutes to, he trudged out of the sleeping quarters and made his way to the tent. As he slipped in beside Harry, a worker he didn't know stood up. Adrian was sitting right at the back of the shed, behind the sister workers and some guy he vaguely remembered as being called Gill or something. Glancing over at the other side of the shed where his parents were, he saw Ella looking at him with a questioning look, but he ignored her. She had become seriously irritating this past year. They used to be close, but he had felt her slipping away from him. Just another thing for him to feel guilty about.

'It's wonderful to see you all here after another year of faithfully keeping on keeping on. I was on a walk this morning, enjoying the birds and just feeling so thankful for everything. I came across another faithful friend, a young person, enjoying the early morning air, seeming so grateful for God's creation. It's so encouraging to see all of the young people you have here, such an encouragement. Welcome everyone, young and old and those in between, to another convention. We'll begin with hymn number …'

Adrian missed the number because he had made eye contact with him. He seemed taller somehow, taller even than yesterday. Adrian concentrated with all his might on his breath, just making it go in and out, barely even hearing the people singing as the whole tent seemed to tilt alarmingly. He put his head in between his legs, vaguely aware of people singing in harmony. Someone singing confidently out of tune. The end of the first hymn. His breath. He tried to breathe. Think of better things. Imagine he was anywhere in the world. Not here. He heard the prayers start. The first sister worker to speak prayed – the words, 'God's love and grace'. Then in a sudden clarity, he heard it all, as though he had been underwater for a few moments. Every noise was suddenly, unbearably loud. A kid moved around and shifted in the seat behind him; the tent was flapping in the light breeze, Harry was breathing too heavily, the grass was making noise outside, someone dropped a pen. He put his hands over his face, his thumbs in his ears and let the tears fall. At least it was acceptable to cry in the meeting.

Ella let the peace of that first hymn wash over her. It felt like a refreshing dip in the ocean to be back in the meeting. She had noticed Adrian walking in late, but she wasn't surprised. Not anymore. He was sitting right beside Guy, though. She was quite jealous of that; she wouldn't have minded being closer to that fine specimen as he had indeed been named the evening before. Justin and her parents were sitting in the row in front of her, a fact that Justin seemed to be delighted with. He kept turning around and smiling at Ella. She loved her little brother with all her heart, but now that he was professing and eleven, this wasn't really appropriate behaviour, so after a couple of times, she frowned at him and pointed towards the workers. She didn't see him much during the conventions, especially in between meetings, as Justin normally just ran around with the other boys his age at convention – just like every other child did unless they were particularly shy, something Justin didn't seem to know the meaning of.

Ella enjoyed the prayers a lot. There were a lot of prayers asking for God to be at the convention. She agreed with this desire. She really felt like this convention was just coming at the right time, especially for Adrian. Of course, she needed it, too, but more importantly she really didn't want to lose her brother to the World. Next came the open prayer time, in which she couldn't hear what anyone was saying, as they didn't use microphones for the friends at prayer time. This was because it was more important that God heard the friends' prayers than that the people around them would, but they still used the mic for the workers.

When Graham prayed for those who were on the fence, stuck in the hedge between the Truth and the world, Ella nearly cried. It was exactly her prayer. She felt it deep inside and prayed along with Graham.

They sang another hymn, by which time Adrian was breathing normally again. He still hadn't moved his head out from between his legs, though. He didn't want to risk seeing him. Harry poked him and he glanced up. He guessed it would be safe enough to look in the opposite direction to the man.

'Are you okay?' Harry whispered.

Adrian didn't even have the energy to lie.

'No.'

'Do you need to leave? You've been crying the whole time so far. I'll come with you if you want.'

Adrian hesitated, but after a moment's thought, he nodded. Harry was such a good friend. As the second hymn started, they both slipped out as the harmonies washed behind them. Adrian didn't look at the other side of the shed. He knew Ella would be frowning at him from a distance. While he loved Ella, he knew she could be seriously judgemental sometimes.

They went for a walk once Adrian had grabbed a couple of tissues from the bathroom. As they left the yard, they ran into a brother worker.

'Where are you lads going? There's a meeting on. Don't be messing about now,' he whispered crossly.

'Mind your own business!' Harry fired back at him.

Harry could be fierce when it counted; Adrian had always admired that about him. They walked out of the yard and onto the quiet road beside the conventions. When they got away from the grounds, Harry turned to Adrian.

'Okay, look, what's going on, Aid. You haven't been yourself at all. I'd say at this convention, but it's actually been a full year at this point. You've lost weight and you're not half as chatty as you were. I'm pretty worried about you. Now you're crying in the meeting. It's too much, I want to help you, but I need to know what it is that is going on with you.'

'It's too much. I don't want to …' Adrian tailed off.

Harry nodded.

'Yeah, it might be too much. I told you about everything though, about being gay, about all of my fears with that … I bared my soul to you that day. I just … I just thought we told each other stuff.'

'We did … We do.' Adrian looked away from his friend.

'So, what is it?'

Adrian paused. 'Can we go to the park? I need to get away from here.'

Harry nodded.

As they rode to the park in silence, Adrian looked out the window. He didn't know how to put these things into words, these nightmares that didn't want to leave him alone. They existed in his head in images, which he tried to block out. They didn't come to him in words. He didn't know what would happen when he moved those images into spoken form. Would they become more powerful? Or would they give him a feeling of control? He supposed he was about to find out.

They got out of the car, feeling the warmth on their skin. They squinted, their eyes adjusting to the sun that was surrounded by an unbroken blue sky.

'It's weird, being out of the meetings when we're at convention,' Harry commented as they made their way to the lake.

'Yeah, we always get into a bubble.' Adrian's voice was still tight and small. 'I always feel funny when we leave to get something for the shop or whatever.'

'Okay. Cut the crap, Adrian. I'll give you time to tell me, but I don't want us to pretend like we're here for no reason.'

Adrian gave a small nod. His jaw clenched, he looked out at a couple of ducks diving close by. 'I hope they catch something,' he said.

'Did you hear what I said?'

'Yes, Harry, I heard what you said.'

'I actually couldn't hear your reply. What did you say?'

Adrian didn't give him an answer. His hands curled at his side as Harry looked at him.

'Is it because I'm gay? Do you have a fear of me?'

Adrian shot a look at Harry. 'Where did you get that idea from?'

'Well, I don't know … You didn't say that you had a problem with it, and you were quite nice at the time, but … maybe you'd changed your mind and you had a revelation about it or something.' Harry's voice got higher as he trailed off.

'It's not that … Also, if someone ever did change their mind about being your friend because of a "revelation", there is something wrong with them, not you.'

He had been shocked out of his anxiety attack to tell him that, but it returned quickly.

'Can we sit?'

'What?'

'Can we sit?'

Harry nodded. They sat and watched the ducks fly off towards trees on the other side of the lake.

'Do you ever wonder where we would be if we hadn't grown up in the meetings?' Adrian broke the silence.

'Well, I would probably not be in the meetings, that's for sure.'

'Makes sense.'

'Yeah. It's not exactly the most gay friendly place ever.' Harry laughed bitterly.

Adrian mustered up a half smile. 'No. It's not.'

The birds continued their chorus, unbothered by the presence of the pair as the young men sat looking out at the lake.

'I was …'

Harry's eyes met Adrian's. 'You were…?' His voice was gentle this time; he had heard something.

'Harry, I—' He didn't know how to tell him this; the words didn't want to come out.
'Fred …'

'Fred?'

'He raped me when I was younger.'

Harry just looked at him.

'He raped me, Harry,' Adrian's eyes filled with tears.

'He raped me, and I couldn't fight against him. I was too weak, I shouldn't have been in his room, I shouldn't have listened to him, I should have screamed, I didn't know.'

Harry was still just looking at him.

'And then he did it again. When I was old enough to fight back. When I could have screamed and could have had Timothy in the room in seconds to see it, could have had him stop … I could have taken him down, Harry – I'm much stronger than him, I could have—'

Harry put his hand on his arm. It tingled.

'Adrian, stop.'

The front of Adrian's T-shirt was getting soaked.

'No, I could have said, *Fred, stop*—'

'Adrian. Stop.' Harry's voice was gentle. 'Stop that. It's not your fault. You could have done those things, but none of that matters because that. Man. Should. Not. Have. Done. That.'

'But I—'

'No, I, he. It's his fault. Please, please, please, stop blaming yourself.'

Adrian nodded wordlessly.

'Can I give you a hug?'

'Yes. I need one.'

The two of them embraced, and Adrian finally felt the edges of his horror soften, just a little. Talking about it had helped his nightmares, he knew that already. He had found his voice.

Chapter Seven

Ella didn't see Adrian leave; she just lifted her head after the hymn and he was gone. She didn't think about it too much. She didn't want to. She just tried to enjoy the meeting. He could make his own choices, she decided. If she focused on his actions, it might ruin her own spirit, and she really just wanted to enjoy this convention. Amy, a young sister worker who had only just joined the work about three years ago, was the first to speak.

'In my field this year,' her voice was shaking, 'we have a family who lost someone in a tragic accident.'

Ella knew the story; she had been shocked when she had heard about a nine-year-old girl who was accidentally run over by a workman on their family farm.

'We were all shocked. We couldn't believe it.'

Ella listened closely, hanging on to every word. These testimonies were more interesting than the rest. They often had a more meaningful message.

'When it happened, we were staying at the grandparents' house, so we heard them get the call. The shock on those poor people's faces was something I'll never forget. The other thing I will never forget is the strength that God gave those people. They were all so strong in the strength of gentleness. When that family was faced with their worst nightmare, any parent or grandparent's worst nightmare, they went to the best source and got help from there.' Amy took a couple of deep breaths, her voice still shaking. 'At the first meeting after everything happened, all that the father of that young girl said was, "I hope that God can use our worst experience to allow someone else to be brought to the way, that one soul would be saved from seeing our hardest experience." I found that so moving – that that was the first wish that the father had after such a traumatic experience. I hope that my own reaction will be the same in every experience; that someone around me would see how I react to such an experience because of how close I am to God. God has a plan with every experience, no matter how awful it is, even if we can't see it while we're in the experience itself. I hope that I can also be thankful for every experience I have.'

Ella was crying at how moving the story was, and saw others around her patting their eyes with tissues. These stories always made her feel a little small when she considered how she reacted to things that happened in her own life sometimes. She felt that she should complain less and thank God more.

In a very strange way that Ella knew was wrong, she had nearly thought that having such an experience, or having left the Truth, would make her testimony more interesting, and therefore more valuable. But she didn't actually want something like that to happen to anyone, never mind those in her family. She had written this in her diary one day and had immediately burned the page just in case someone would find the entry and think she actually wanted to leave the Truth or that she wanted someone to be hurt.

David, the second worker of the convention, spoke after Amy.

'We are all on a path. Some of us are on the path to heaven, and, although we don't like to think of it, some of us are on the path to an eternity empty of God. There are two paths spoken about in the Bible: the way that is broad and many travel; and the way that is straight and narrow. I know that there are many who are on the broad way, those around us, maybe even family members stuck on this way, not seeing that it just leads to sorrow and loss, but there is a better way. The way that leads to heaven and to our home, as that hymn that we just sang says. This is the way we should all want to be on. It may seem harder and not worth it as we continue on, but it is always worth it, no matter the cost. We just heard about the family who lost such an important member, and while that is the worst imaginable thing to lose, it does remind us that on the narrow way, we have to let go of earthly things.' He finished by saying, 'And I hope that we can all remain on the narrow way until the end of days when we reach that final shore.'

It was something Ella had heard many times before, but it meant even more when Adrian seemed to be on his way out. She wanted to tell him to listen, but he wasn't there. It was a shame, as it could help him understand that the path he was heading down was dangerous.

The time for testimony came and went – when the friends could stand and tell their own thoughts from the year into the mic – and while a lot of people stood up, some of them spoke for so long that a few people couldn't actually speak. Ella had always found this very rude, as speaking for an extended period of time meant that fewer people could speak and that those who were waiting to speak were having to stand in front of four hundred-plus people for maybe fifteen minutes. Ella had been in that position and she disliked it a lot. Plus, those people rarely had anything interesting to share. Secretly, she had a theory that they just liked the sound of their own voices.

Graham spoke of a few different things, but the biggest thing that Ella took away from what he said was his modesty speech. He spoke of how the friends in Canada had slowly let the devil slip into how they were dressing. He told the girls that it was a good thing to stand out from the world with longer skirts, despite what the current fashions of the world were. He told them they shouldn't dress as men with jeans and trousers. He said that a modest woman was a beautiful thing, that the friends and sister workers were the most beautiful women in the world, as they had Jesus and were full of the holy spirit. Ella was glad she had listened to her mother, as she could see some people looking quite uncomfortable with what he was saying.

He did comment on heels, though, saying that high heels were becoming all too common, which he described as vanity and vexation of the spirit. Ella decided she'd wear flats tomorrow. He also spoke about the dangers of the internet. He said that there were people out in the world and on the internet who were looking to question the Truth, and that those people were of the devil, trying to lead other people astray. Ella had never thought of googling the friends and didn't even know there was anything on the internet about the friends. This revelation never left her, but she pushed down the newfound curiosity. She now knew that it was dangerous, thankfully.

After the meeting was over, Ella remembered that Adrian had disappeared. She decided she'd look for him after and ask him what was going on. In the meantime, she had to eat as she had four tables to clear up. Normally it was two, but they were short on help; a lot of people just came and didn't help out with any of the jobs, choosing to stand or sit on the benches outside and talk to their friends instead. At dinner time, Ella ended up sitting between Hannah and a couple of middle-aged ladies, who were talking about their friend who had lost a mother in the last couple of weeks.

'Yeah, I can't believe she's had to go through that, just after her two kids stopped professing as well.'

'Such a hard thing to go through, especially when her mum wasn't even professing either.'

'I know, I was trying to comfort her, but you just can't give her false hope – of course she knows the reality. I would hate to think of my own mother going to a lost eternity.'

'Yeah, the funeral was at the church. She wanted the workers to hold the funeral, but her two other siblings refused. A couple of the workers went to the funeral. I was there, too, of course.'

'I would have gone but I had to babysit my grandson.'

'He's getting so big!' They continued talking among themselves.

Ella stopped listening, turning to Hannah to talk about their plans for the summer. Hannah was going to Nigeria to meet her grandparents for the first time in her memory. She had been born there, but they had moved when she was just two. Her parents had already known that they wanted to move to Ireland when she was born, so she had got an English name compared to her brothers, Akin and Debare. This was apparently to allow her to integrate into the culture, but as Hannah said, if she could pronounce Irish, they should be able to pronounce Nigerian names.

The plans were that Hannah would travel with one of the workers and then come back with a different Irish worker who would be returning to Ireland. All the workers who went abroad to preach the gospel came back at least every five years to visit family. They generally didn't come back themselves in the time in between, even if someone in their family died, unless they were a sister worker coming back to care for a parent, or if they got sick and needed to come home for expert care they could only get in Ireland. Hannah was very excited.

'I can't wait, one set lives in Lagos, and the others live just outside Lagos. I have heard that Lagos is incredibly busy, but if I stick with the friends, it should be okay.' Hannah's whole face lit up as she told Ella stories of her grandparents that she had heard from her own parents over the years. Hannah's maternal grandparents had visited her a few years ago. Ella had met them and found Hannah's grandmother a fascinating storyteller. She had sat and listened to her for hours on end. Hannah's paternal grandparents were apparently poorer and therefore had never been over to visit, so now Hannah would meet them for the first time in her living memory.

'I'm really looking forward to that – I wonder what they'll be like,' she said, her smile splitting her face in two. She told Ella about all her favourite meals her mother made her that were apparently better in Nigeria, like jollof rice with chicken which they got for birthdays and special occasions and suya. Her parents couldn't join her for the full four weeks, but they would join her for two weeks in the middle. This was why Hannah would be travelling without them.

They discussed other plans for the summer. Hannah would be missing the yearly tradition of all the friends going to the beach, playing volleyball, and having barbeques. She was sad about this, but they planned to meet up and go on a camping trip later in the year. Older than Ella and Grace, at nineteen, Hannah could now drive and was going to be designated driver for the next couple of years. Ella was planning on learning to drive, but it was all so expensive. She had planned on starting lessons in the summer, though. Hannah also lived quite close to Ella compared to Grace, who lived two hours away from the other two.

Ella hadn't seen Adrian in a while now, she realised as she was wiping her third table, getting slightly fed up with the feeling of salt and jam on her hand. The cloths they were given to wipe the table with were single use and not great quality. They didn't disguise the texture of the materials she was cleaning very well, making the task unpleasant. She considered looking for her brother, but decided to concentrate on the task at hand first. She glanced up as Azi, Hannah's dad, walked over to her and Hannah.

'Hello, ladies,' he said in his deep voice, smiling at them.

They exchanged greetings, both girls immersed in the task at hand.

'Can I speak to you, my daughter?' He gestured to a table nearby. Hannah nodded and followed her dad over to a table, presumably to get out of earshot of Ella.

Continuing with her job, Ella purposefully didn't listen in, but out of the corner of her eye, she could see Hannah looking first angry, and then scared as Azi's voice became louder and his gestures wider.

One of the workers on the staff of the convention whom Ella didn't know as well appeared beside her, making her jump.

'It is good when our parents chide us – it keeps us humble and shows us that they love us.'

Ella turned towards the worker, an elderly lady who Ella knew was prone to say some more controversial things.

'I don't think what is happening there is any of our business.' She turned away from the worker, confused about the resentment she was feeling towards the lady. After all, the older lady was a worker sent from God. Ella should respect her.

Hannah was starting to look quite scared, though, so Ella finished her job quickly and walked over to the two with a smile on her face.

'Hey, Azi, I'm so sorry to interrupt, but I need Hannah to help me finish up. Will you be much longer?'

'No, I just have to discuss one more thing with my daughter and she will be all yours,' Azi said, giving Ella a tight-lipped smile as his eyes flashed something unreadable at his daughter.

Ella nodded and glanced at Hannah, who smiled slightly too brightly at her. Walking over to the cookhouse, she grabbed some bread out of the cupboard and considered what that worker had said. She knew what the best thing for a child was to listen and obey your parents. The conversations she had had with Hannah about her father previously, though, had seemed hard for Hannah to bear.

Where was the line, Ella wondered, between the punishments your parents give you because they loved you, and pure cruelty.

Adrian, meanwhile, was on a walk with Harry. They strolled through the park together, neither of them speaking much. What the next step was, they weren't sure. You couldn't really just leave the convention without having to come up with a reasonable explanation for leaving. They had discussed their options, and Adrian didn't want to tell the police about what had happened. He did want to talk to someone, however, a 'real adult', as they called them. Suddenly, he thought of his grandmother. He had her number. He barely ever used it, but he had a feeling that she was probably his best bet, so he gave her a call.

'Hello?' She sounded confused.

'Hi, Grandma? This is Adrian.'

'Adrian?' Now she sounded really confused.

'Could I ask you something?'

'Of course.'

Adrian never went back to the convention grounds; neither did Harry. Ella didn't find out what had happened that day

for a while and didn't ask him either. If she were honest
with herself, she knew she didn't want to know what had
led him out just in case it would lead her out as well.

The rest of Saturday felt like it flew by for Ella.
Once her mother had located Adrian and found out that he
wasn't coming back, knew he was safe and wasn't going to
tell them why he had just left, they just decided to settle in
and worry about his absence later, otherwise his absence
would ruin the whole convention. The rest of the day
followed a similar routine, except the last meeting was
slightly shorter than the rest of the meetings had been.

The next day was a Sunday, the biggest day of the
whole convention. Ella was gradually getting more nervous
for that evening. She wore a blue dress, her favourite,
which didn't need too many additions as it came up to her
neck, covered her shoulders, and wasn't see-through. She
happened to match her friends as well, who were both
wearing blue: Hannah in a blue dress and Grace in a blue
skirt. It was colder and raining, back to typical Irish
weather, so they all added denim jackets with coats over
the top. Hannah's hairstyle of choice was a donut bun,
while Ella's hair still wasn't cooperating, so she just plaited
it.

Sunday, like Saturday, went by in a flurry of
meetings and chatting in between until the last meeting.
Ella felt time warping as it came closer to the time. She
was certain she stank of sweat but couldn't smell it under
her armpits. She had spoken to Timothy Farmer – the
overseer of the workers in Ireland – yesterday and he had
agreed that she could take the step. Now that she had told
him, it was official. She had read all the verses which he

had suggested. After she had taken this step, she would definitely be going to heaven. Ella wasn't certain but she thought that maybe if she weren't baptised, she wouldn't go to heaven … She didn't really want to leave anything up to chance. Better to be baptised than not, though. This step would mean that she could take the bread and wine every Sunday morning meeting. It also meant that she would have to die to self every day for the rest of her life, but she would worry about that later.

Now all she had to do was stand up at the right time, in the right place, in front of the right five hundred people and then tomorrow it would happen. She'd definitely maybe get into heaven now. If she managed to continue faithfully until the end. Either way, she'd get a nice beef pie for dinner tomorrow, a nice change from stew, bread, and porridge – the normal food for convention. She arrived in the meeting eight minutes early; she would have gone earlier but she got caught up in the pre-meeting line to the toilets. She sat down, her hands trembling and sweating so much she could hardly hold her Bible and hymnbook. Her heart was racing. She tried to breathe normally. The wind was howling outside and it was pouring with rain. Grace and Hannah were dripping either side of her, having been caught in the deluge.

The sides of the tent were flapping, drowning out much of what people were saying. Time felt like it forgot all the rules. Then, suddenly, the moments were flying past, and the worker was standing up and he was speaking. She struggled to hear what he was saying, even though he was talking louder than usual.

'Welcome back to another meeting. Before we begin, I have been asked to request that anyone who feels moved to be baptised to stand up. Baptism is an important step. It shows that you are willing to die to self every day, no matter what. It is something that should be taken very seriously. So, if anyone is feeling moved and willing, if they could stand up now?'

Somehow her legs had the strength to bear her weight as she stood up. She felt movement either side of her and realised that Grace and Hannah were also getting baptised. They all sat down when they knew that the worker had seen them.

'Thank you. Can those getting baptised and their families stay after the meeting tomorrow morning.'

Chapter Eight

The next morning, Ella had her baptism clothes set out on her bed, as did Grace and Hannah. A sister worker they knew pretty well had come up to them and their parents just after the meeting and had told them to collect old clothes that were very modest. The girls had talked about today ever since they had all stood up. None of them had had any idea the others would be getting baptised, although, on reflection, none of them had spoken much that afternoon before the meeting, each of them having been stuck in their own worlds. That evening, at eleven, they had been shushed when they were still whispering excitedly about it all.

After a very slow meeting that felt like it lasted longer than the whole convention had, Ella, Grace, and Hannah stayed back, along with a couple of guys Ella had vaguely known her whole life. They gathered quietly, all nervous. A few workers also joined. They were told to meet the rest of them at the baptism pool, an old pool beside the convention grounds. Ella had seen this pool before they'd cleaned it out and she was not hugely excited about being dunked into it. It looked kind of cold.

The three girls, their mothers, and a couple of other relatives went down to the sleeping quarters. Ella had her granny and aunt there as well. The mothers and other family members were chatting happily, but none of the girls to be baptised were talking. They grabbed their old clothes and were given a few other items.

When they were finished, Ella's clothes included:

-A swimming suit

-An old long-sleeved top

-A pair of thick black tights

-A long old skirt lent to her by her grandmother who lived in the area

-A thick jumper

-A coat that went down to her calves given to her by the workers

The workers used big pins to attach her skirt to her long coat. She decided once she had all the layers on that she wasn't going to be cold after all. Her friends were dressed similarly. None of them had actually been to a baptism before. They knew that at other conventions in different countries, everyone attended – Ella had met someone who had been watched by a thousand people as they got into the water. In Ireland, however, it was a small affair, for which Ella was grateful, although she wouldn't have minded having prior knowledge of the process at this point.

When they left the sleeping quarters, it felt like they were already in the pool, the rain was coming down so hard. Ella would have made a joke about this, but she knew that this was such a serious occasion and therefore not the time for jokes. She would maybe attempt it later if she remembered. The girls didn't talk. The mothers carried towels down to the baptism area for them along with their hymnbooks for the hymns they would sing, holding big umbrellas over their heads to prevent everything from getting wet. Their wellies sank as they trudged over the wet ground, newly soaked after the dry spell. They stood under the umbrellas, unsure, as a worker said something almost no one could hear.

Apparently someone could hear him, though, as they started singing. Anna scrambled for the hymn, guessing wildly, but as there were only three baptism hymns, it wasn't too hard. Someone behind them was harmonising with the hymn as they stood around the water, a small group all bowed against the cold and wet. Ella could barely sing. She was shivering from anticipation and nerves. This whole experience felt a bit embarrassing. It didn't help that she was dressed in the most unattractive way possible. While she had trained herself to not care too much about how she looked, she wasn't comfortable with actively looking as unattractive as possible. With a good bit of effort, though, she shoved those feelings to the back of her head. This would all be worth it when they reached the hallowed shores.

Another worker said something else Ella couldn't catch, and suddenly she was gently being prodded forwards. The girls looked at one another, wordlessly trying to decide who should go first. Ella wanted this whole experience over with. It had been wholly unpleasant up to this point and there was no point in dragging the wait out. Better to get the peace with God faster. She walked forwards as a different brother worker dressed in an old shirt and trousers got into the pool. She stepped down cautiously, helped by the worker so she wouldn't slip. As she didn't know the depths of the pool, Ella found this helpful. The worker was somewhere between middle aged and old and someone she didn't really know. She just knew he was boring in the meetings. He quietly told her where to stand.

'Trust me, I'm not going to drop you,' he whispered.

Ella nodded.

'I baptise you in the name of the Father, the Son and the Holy Spirit,' he shouted.

He brought Ella backwards, and gently lowered her body, then her head under the water. She resisted panicking as the water flowed over her nose and mouth. Then he immediately brought her up again. It was freezing.

'Thank you,' she said as he helped her out.

He nodded slightly, moving as her mother and aunt grabbed her hand and covered her in her towel, produced by a sister worker hiding behind a large umbrella. She had taken the towels as they had arrived to keep them dry. Ella then stood and shivered while Hannah went through the same process, followed by Grace, then the two lads, who were simply wearing old shirts and old trousers. She envied the simplicity of their outfits. When it was all over, they sang another hymn and walked back to the showers.

The one thing she never forgot from that moment was that all she felt was cold and nervous. There was no immediate peace from the process. She felt nothing until they were showered and back in their normal clothes, walking up to the dining shed to eat. At that point, she felt the wave of peace, which only lasted for a few moments as she joined those who were already there. She was last up, so her friends were already eating. Being baptised was hungry work, so she ate with gusto and integrated back into the normal conversations. There was no conversation about what it had meant, so Ella still felt slightly confused about the whole process, but she did enjoy the pies. She missed the peace, though, and would have liked to discuss it. Considering the reason for the lack of peace was scary. What if it meant that she was going to have to go in the work? She'd worry about it later.

The next meeting, those who had been baptised were asked to share their testimony. Ella felt nervous again when they were singing the hymn, but stood up with Grace and Hannah, once again amazed at her legs' abilities to stand. She waited while the guys spoke first, then Grace, and then it was her turn. She didn't have a lot to say.

'I'm really thankful to be able to be here once again. I have been thinking a lot about Noah and his faith in serving God. Even though everyone around him was persecuting him. Noah kept on with his project; he knew that God would deliver. Sometimes the world can be a bit like that – that they wonder why we are doing all that we do, but we know that if we prevail, God will help us to build our ark for the end so we don't perish in the destruction of the Earth. I long that I would be better at following God's commands and being precise with how I do things depending on how God has asked me to do them. I long to be able to focus more on what God wants and to ignore the distractions and disbelief of those around me. I also long to be a good example to those around, that they would see something special in my life and that they don't just see someone building an ark just for the show, that I would be a quiet example to a lost soul. I hope that God will help me with this.'

'Amen' echoed around the tent.

She sat down and took a breath. Perfect peace.
Maybe she wouldn't have to go in the work after all. She
enjoyed what Hannah said about Moses being faithful with
being willing to sacrifice his son.

That meeting and the next passed quickly and, once
they had finished their jobs, it was time to have the sing.
They all sat in a messy semicircle around the meeting tent,
none of them sitting in their normal seats. A particularly
good singer started the hymns, and they all gave out the
hymns that were speaking to them at that moment or which
they just enjoyed the harmonies of. Ella truly loved these
moments – these were the memories she would think of for
the rest of the year to keep herself in the right spirit. They
had heard about how they should be little children in the
last meeting, how they shouldn't let too much of
themselves in. They should submit themselves wholly unto
God. These thoughts were going to be Ella's aim for this
year, she had decided. A half-hearted, lukewarm sacrifice
wasn't enough.

The last speaker in that meeting had spoken about
the end of times. This was something that they heard about
quite regularly in the meetings, but it was something that
Ella was finally okay with. She had struggled with truly
accepting the world's ending for a long time or even just
dying suddenly. She hadn't really wanted to die at her
young age, and had felt that she wanted to live a lot more
of her life before that time. But, this last day of convention,
she finally felt that she would be okay if she had to die that
evening. It was giving her a peace beyond all
understanding. She had thought that there was something
wrong with her for not being willing to die, as it was talked

about so often. She knew of course that the reward at the end would be worth it, but for some reason she had never truly been able to make peace with it. Now, though, she had perfect peace about it. She hoped that the peace about it would last forever. It was better to be ready for it, as they never knew when Jesus would come back.

Tuesday, like the rest of the convention, flew. All too soon, it was time for clear-up. Ella had made small talk with Guillermo a few more times, but he had started showing interest in a popular girl, so she had given up on him as a prospective relationship. She helped with the clear-up for a while, but they had to get on the road as they had a long journey ahead of them. She said her emotional goodbyes, wishing Hannah all the best with her time in Nigeria. Ella's dad was yelling for her, so she sped up the last goodbyes.

'You have to come with me someday!'

'I would love that – maybe in a few years we'll make a trip out there together. This time, though, try out all the dishes your mum goes on about and let us know how good they really are!'

'Yeah, I'll do that, and I'll try to take photos and notes of all the good places we can visit together!'

Peter honked the horn. Ella hugged Grace and Hannah tightly and turned towards the car as she spoke. 'Sorry, if I wait any longer my dad will just drive off without me. I love you both!'

Hannah and Grace nodded. They both knew Peter had to get back for his work that evening and was stressing about it.

'No problem, go on.'

'I'll call you both!' She sprinted down to the car and clambered in, trying not to focus on the fact that she had a spare seat beside her now. Her mum turned round.
'Did you kids have a nice convention?'

Chapter Nine

Ella was busy. Between her part-time job in a local produce shop, she went to a yearly gathering of the friends, then she was going on hikes and staying with her best friends, and in August they were going on a family holiday to Greece. The whole summer was already booked up and she had barely eaten her first ice cream.

The week at the beach was fun. The friends had walked down the town, greeting one another, observing new relationships and gossiping about everything. Ella loved it. They had spent a lot of time in the sea or playing volleyball and trying to figure out if it was the brethren or the friends. Walks on the beach at sunset with sightings of handsome single guys of her age, Ella was in her element. And, to top off the whole experience, she spent it with Grace. They were missing Hannah a lot, of course, but she was apparently having the time of her life in Nigeria according to the emails they got from her. Sometimes the three went long periods without seeing one another anyway, so having conventions and then the beach week within weeks of each other was a once-a-year occurrence. As they lived further away from the beach, her family didn't always make the journey for a week that was generally specifically the Northern friends' gathering. This was probably because just having a southern registration on your car could cause stones to be thrown at you if some people in dodgy areas were in the wrong mood. In fact, most southerners avoided the North on 12 July. This time, however, Adrian was going up and he was bringing Ella with him. They were staying at the house with Grace's family and it was so much fun. They barely slept, obviously, but they had a lot of good times and rarely woke up before eleven.

Adrian and her parents, and for some reason their grandparents as well, had had a conversation. They had changed the way they acted around him a little bit, but they had seemed to have made up after convention. So, Ella didn't dwell on it too long. It was probably about how he had left the convention, she reasoned.

Two weeks later, Ella was going up her first Wicklow Mountain with some of the friends. Grace had driven to Ella's house, then Grace, Ella, and Adrian made their way in Adrian's little Clio up the winding roads. They arrived in a car park to a group of people standing waiting for them. They were late, as usual. They clambered out of the car and grabbed their hiking gear. Ella had had to ask her brother what she needed to pack, as she had literally never climbed a mountain before. The two girls had debated about what to wear the night before. They had both settled on wearing a loose knee-length skirt with a pair of shorts underneath. Ella felt slightly self-conscious as she noticed that the older girls were wearing leggings. She stood outside the circle, behind Grace who joined in the conversation naturally. Once Adrian was ready, they all started out. Ella wasn't unfit – having to play sport regularly at school had kept her fitness to a reasonable level – but she had never climbed a mountain before, so was caught unaware when they started along a relatively steep path up through a forest.

'Hey, I don't think I've met you before. I'm Sarah.' A tall girl with red hair combed back into a ponytail fell into step with her.

'Hey,' breathed Ella. 'Sorry, I'm more unfit than I thought, not able to talk right now.'

'Oh, that's normal,' laughed Sarah, 'I'd say you're just in your first wind.'

'First …' puff … 'wind?'

'Yeah, it takes a little while to get your stride but I'd say you'll cope better in a little while. I used to get it too, but now I'm up these mountains every other day, so I'm now used to it.'

That explained a lot.

'That makes me feel a lot better,' Ella laughed, relaxing. She had spent the last few days worrying about not being fit enough for the mountain and this inability to walk without having to puff and pant had worried her.

They chatted on, Ella eventually managing to keep the pace of the group pretty well and getting to know some of the friends she had never met as they always ended up at different conventions. It was a big enough group. There were about twenty of them in total, but they split off into smaller groups naturally. They joined back together at lunch time. Ella was starving when they finally stopped for lunch. It was only half twelve, but she could have eaten an hour ago. They sat down on various stones and a couple just sat cross-legged on the ground. They all gave thanks inwardly and then sat around eating. Ella was sitting beside a cute guy she had seen at the beach that year.

'Hey, I'm David.'

'I'm Ella, I think I saw you at the beach a couple of weeks ago?'

'Oh aye, I think I recognise you from there too. Are you from around here?'

'No, I live about an hour away from here, yourself?'

'Ah right, I'm from about three hours from here, I live up in the north on a wee farm so I do.'

'Oh wow, that's quite the run! What brings you all this way?'

'Ah, I enjoy the craic, you know yourself. What about you?'

'My brother,' she pointed at Adrian, 'brought us – we thought it would be fun to come for the ride.'

'What animals do you have?' Ella asked, interrupting his second bite of his ham roll.

'Oh, we keep a few cattle and a couple of sheep, just for the craic, you know yourself.'

Ella didn't, but she nodded anyway. They chatted for the rest of the lunch and continued on the walk, falling behind the rest of the group, engaged in the conversation. She learned a few things about him, his three sisters and his life on the farm. He was full of fascinating stories about days spent chasing livestock around fields and helping new life come into the world. He wanted to be a vet and just had one more year of school left before he could start studying for his dream. He was busy trying to arrange placements, as he needed to have a certain amount of experience on farms that weren't his own before he could study veterinary medicine in Ireland. He had already spent some time on a pig farm and told Ella a hilarious story about being chased by a sow that had noticed the sandwich he was holding. Ella laughed at all the right moments and then told David about George and his misguided efforts to catch Hannah's attention. They talked the whole way down the mountain and shared a lift as they went over to one of the friends' houses for some takeout and games.

That evening, before Ella left for home, she got David's number. She was buzzing. He was cute and she found him fascinating with all of his stories of growing up on the farm. Her excitement was interrupted though when Adrian teased her mercilessly about him on the car ride home.

Adrian had enjoyed his hike as much as Ella, but Harry wasn't there and he was missing him. Adrian was starting to think about Harry more and more, in ways that, if his parents could read his mind, would definitely get him kicked out of the house. Adrian would be going to the same university as Harry that September, so he was looking forward to that. He hadn't told Harry about his feelings, though, as he wasn't really sure what they meant and their relationship had already been altered plenty by their conversation that day at convention. Harry was now Adrian's protector and wouldn't let anyone hurt him, having taken a protective stance during the conversation between his parents and grandparents.

Harry was so angry about what Fred had done to him. Adrian's parents had acted oddly, though. They'd listened to him, but they didn't really come across as if they had believed him. They hadn't gone to the police, as they said it would be better if they tried to talk to Fred first and see if they could maybe get the workers to sort it out themselves. Adrian's grandparents had fought against this idea, stating outright that the police needed to know, or Fred would keep doing this to other children whose houses he was staying at.

That had caused a debate, in which his dad had repeated the phrase, 'I'm the father and this is my decision to make'. His grandparents had left in a terrible mood, and Adrian had felt awful about it. His stomach, which had hurt regularly since he was eight, was really playing up since his grandparents left and hadn't really settled since. He had been to the doctors about it and had had tests to make sure it wasn't a stomach ulcer or anything more sinister, but everything had come back clear – which was both a blessing and a curse. It did mean, however, that he still didn't have an answer for it.

Adrian's mind drifted as he teased Ella, thinking about the last conversation he had had with Harry. Harry had told him he wasn't going to go to meetings anymore and Adrian was a bit troubled with that revelation. He didn't agree with most of the things the workers said, but he still believed that the way was the only way and that he might go to hell if he didn't profess anymore. It was all so complicated.

'There are just so many things I don't agree with, Aid – like why are your parents not letting you go to the police? And why can the women not wear trousers if they feel like it? And why, as a gay man, must I pretend to be someone I'm not just to make people feel more comfortable with my existence within the friends. In the meantime, they speak about loving everyone and forgiveness with those same mouths they slag people like me off with. I just don't buy it anymore. I don't mind if you still want to go to meetings – we can just not talk about meeting stuff – but I'm just so fed up with all the bullshit.'

It was the first time that Adrian had heard Harry swear and it gave him a weird feeling in his stomach. Everything seemed to go to his stomach these days.

Chapter Ten

The meeting with Fred was arranged for a couple of weeks before Adrian was meant to move to Dublin for college. Adrian paced around the house, cried in the bathroom, vomited, and didn't sleep for the three days leading up to it. He called in sick to work and just got himself into such a state he didn't even shower. The morning of the meeting, Anna came into his room and ordered him out of bed and into the shower.

'You stink,' she said as he trudged to the bathroom.

'Gee, thanks, mam,' he muttered as he followed her orders.

When Fred and Timothy arrived (Timothy was the overseer, or head worker, of the region), they all sat around the table. Adrian was already sitting at the table across from the men.

'Anyone want any tea?' Anna fussed, putting out pastries and buns that she'd got from the local bakery.

'Yes, I would,' both Fred and Timothy replied, and she came out a short time later with four cups, as Adrian had refused. He had known anything that went in at the moment would probably come straight out again. He just looked down at his hands as they chatted about the weather.

'I couldn't believe it when I looked outside,' Peter was saying. 'It had been such good weather just five minutes before and then it was pouring down. Of course, that was the day that I'd forgotten my umbrella.'

'I had him nearly chased out of here, the amount he was dripping on the floor,' Anna added.

The conversation moved on to those in the fields that the workers had been in. Anna and Peter filled Fred in on a couple of halls in the area that they could use for the gospel meetings.

'The meetings will hopefully be starting in about a month or so, I think,' Fred told them.

'Oh lovely, we look forward to that, don't we, Peter,' said Anna and Peter nodded.

Adrian's hands were red where he was picking them between his thumb and forefinger.

'Stop that, Adrian,' Anna whispered, poking him.

He stopped and mumbled that he was going to the toilet. He stood in the bathroom and leaned against the cold radiator in an attempt to distract himself from his stomach cramps. There was no part of him that wanted to go back into that room. Still, he felt his legs bring him back, felt himself manage a half smile at Timothy, and somehow he was back in the room. Sitting across from his abuser.

Adrian felt glued to the chair, wanting to leave, until there was a lull in the conversation.

'So, I think we all know why we have asked you to come here.' Peter started. The air in the room suddenly changed. Adrian felt the impact of a sudden lack of oxygen.

'We do. I can't believe your boy would accuse me of something so serious,' Fred answered. Adrian couldn't see the expression on his face as he was refusing to look up.

'Well, we can't understand why he would lie about it,' Anna replied.

'No, I'm sure you can't, but I think you will agree that this *man*, and I may call him that as he is eighteen, that he does not have the best track record. He left the convention, I heard, and has been missing meetings recently.'

'He is just about a man, and we are talking about things that happened years ago.' Anna sounded angry. Adrian hoped that she would do most of the talking and he could just survive the ordeal.

'Yes yes, well what I am most interested in is what he himself has to say for himself. Spreading lies about a worker, I think it is unacceptable. Are you going to apologise, Adrian?'

Adrian was shocked into looking up.

'You are the one who is lying. You abused me when I was too young to fight back, and recently you used your previous power over me to get me into that helpless state again. You are perverse and you did it when Timothy here was in the next room. I never want to have to see your face again. Mum, Dad, I can't cope with this. I'm leaving.' He walked out of the room.

'You see, he can't even stick with his lies,' he heard Fred's smooth reply.

Adrian ran upstairs and locked himself in the bathroom, and vomited. He collapsed on the floor, his stomach in agony. He felt like howling, but he just felt numb. He had forgotten the abuse for so long – it was so buried that it was hurting a lot to bring it all up, with the latest incident on top of it.

A short while later, he heard footsteps come up the stairs.

'Adrian …' Timothy's voice floated through the door, gentle.

A pause. He didn't want to reply.

'Yes.' His body did it anyway.

'Can I talk to you for a second?'

Adrian shook his head inwardly, but once again, his body took over, and he was standing up, dabbing his eyes and opening the door. He sat down, though, as his body stopped working on its own and he turned his back on the enabler.

'Look … we don't want you to harden your heart over this.' Timothy sighed. 'I don't completely disbelieve what you are telling me.'

Adrian half turned his head towards him. *Very generous*, he thought.

'But, Adrian, I don't want you mentioning it again … You … I know you're doing all you know to, but you are disrupting the peace of the people.' A pause. He wanted Adrian to say something, it seemed. When no response came, he continued. 'We all make mistakes Adrian, you know that. We are a perfect way, not a perfect people. No one knows that more than I. But I want you to pray hard, pray about your future actions and how you react to people in the future.' He put his hand on Adrian's shoulder, and Adrian flinched.

'Just remember, Adrian, your parents had this meeting to help you to come back to the way. We actually had an interesting conversation with them since, and I hope that this conversation today has sown a seed in both of your hearts.'

Adrian didn't reply. Once again, Timothy stood there in silence, waiting. When that didn't come, he put his hand back on Adrian's shoulder. Adrian shook him off this time, resisting the urge to slap him.

'Please don't be so hard, soften your heart and you will see the way clear again.'

He took a step or two towards the staircase and paused for a second before continuing. Adrian heard the footsteps get quieter as Timothy walked back down the stairs. Adrian banged his head against the tiles softly, moaning.

Anna and Peter waved their visitors off when it seemed that Adrian wasn't going to come back downstairs. They stood at the door, arms wrapped around each other as the workers drove off.

'Well, I think that was productive.' Peter commented as he released his wife and started walking towards the living room. Anna just nodded. She stood at the front door, thinking of her son's back retreating out of that room. Fred had brushed it off, of course he had, and Anna wanted to support the workers no matter what, but she worried about her son. She went upstairs and looked for him in his room. He wasn't there. She walked towards the bathroom and stood outside. She heard her son's anguish through the door. She walked towards her own bedroom and sat on the side of her bed and buried her head in her hands.

Chapter Eleven

Adrian was moving in across the street from Harry into a small room in a house in Dublin. His parents, Ella, and Justin helped him move all his belongings in – not that he had many, but it was helpful to have the moral support of his family. He was kind of nervous, but he was glad that he wasn't going to have to go to the gospel meeting with Fred. He wasn't feeling hugely excited to go to any meeting or gospel meeting these days, but he didn't say this to his parents or siblings. He hadn't said much to his parents at all since the meeting with the workers. He kind of wanted to forget that incident.

When they had moved most of the luggage in the right places, they all went out for lunch. At the restaurant, Adrian saw familiar shapes in the corner, waving at them.

'Surprise!' Anna turned to Adrian, beaming. 'We arranged for the workers to come and visit us all here so we could all have a nice conversation with them.'

Harry blinked.

'Do you think there is any way I can leave that doesn't look rude right now?' he whispered to Adrian.

Adrian shook his head.

'Sorry, I don't think so, buddy. If I did, I'd be using it first.' He had told Harry about the visit, who had been utterly disgusted with how they'd handled it.

Anna and Ella hugged Dana and Katie, while the men all shook their hands. They smiled at Harry uncertainly. Small talk was made as they congratulated Adrian on his new place at university.

Harry shifted as they sat waiting for the waiter to bring them over to the table with the workers. He had painted his nails recently and you could see the outline of the nail varnish on the edges of his nails. Even though he had taken the polish off before Adrian's parents had turned up, there was still an obvious trace of what had been there.

'It's great that you're going to be living so close to the Sunday evening gospel meeting, and the morning meeting! It'll be so easy for you to get there.' Anna looked genuinely excited.

'Yeah, no excuses now,' Peter joked, and everyone apart from Harry and Adrian laughed. Adrian had really wanted to have excuses and it felt like they were tearing them away from him, one by one. The rest of the dinner thankfully went without any drama, but neither Adrian nor Harry had enjoyed it.

That Sunday, Adrian was hungover. It had been his first-ever party with alcohol and he turned out to be a lightweight. After one beer he was already tipsy, and properly drunk after three. He didn't enjoy the alcohol that much, nor the feeling of being drunk, but he was determined to defy his parents as much as possible, even if they didn't know about it. He was mostly just angry after that dinner, especially after what had happened just two weeks before. Adrian and Harry had been blindsided by the workers' presence and had had to make stupid conversation about nothing that mattered instead of enjoying his last evening with his family. He was getting seriously fed up with the whole set-up. They had done that to try and make him feel more guilty if he didn't go to meetings, and Adrian did not appreciate the blatant manipulation tactics.

They had also made Harry feel incredibly uncomfortable, with several comments about temptations and how God gives them battles and tests and how everyone needed to avoid these tests or they would fall into the devil's trap. Adrian had had to sit with Harry as he cried later that evening. He told Adrian that he'd felt that he was wrong his whole life and questioned why a God that was all-loving would give someone such a big obstacle to overcome.

'I tried … so hard, Adrian, so hard … to just be straight. To like girls, to suppress my own personality. I can't do it anymore. Those people think I am wrong just for the gender I am attracted to, for wanting to be myself. They tell us we have to suppress ourselves, but I think that the people who say that have never had to do it themselves.' He had sobbed, in a foetal position at the end of Adrian's bed.

It broke Adrian's heart to see this, once again, affecting his best friend so intensely. Adrian had thought about his own feelings and how he thought he might be bisexual, but he hadn't told Harry this at that point. Instead, he held his childhood best friend and felt helpless as he saw their upbringing drag him down so much. He was feeling so unbelievably angry at those workers, at their feelings of self-righteousness that had led them to give their opinions in the first place. Shame washed over him when the thought of what his own opinion had been back the first time Harry had told him about the biggest secret he had, which brought him the most shame. He felt utterly lost as he suddenly realised he might not be able to ever have the same relationship with his parents again if he told them that he was bisexual. He couldn't comprehend what that might mean for his future life. At that moment, however, he wasn't that fond of his parents. Especially when he thought of what they had done to him. How could they arrange a meeting with the worker who had abused him? And then pretend like nothing had happened? Their handling of the situation disgusted him.

They had kissed last night, Adrian suddenly remembered. He had held Harry's face in his hands and they had kissed, their tears adding to the taste of booze on each other's lips. With that thought, he stood up and glanced at his phone which was still ringing with the goddamn alarm. Nine am. Two hours to the meeting.

Ella was at David's house that weekend. They had been texting for a month already. Anna had brought Ella halfway to David's house and David had picked her up from there. They were getting on really well, and Ella thought he might kiss her when they went out to feed the stock. He didn't, but she could feel the chemistry between them building. He was so cute in his farm clothes, with a checked shirt and jeans with his wellies. They could talk about all sorts of things. She knew, for example, that he wanted four kids which matched her number of between three and four. She also knew he was really excited to be a vet, but that he dreaded the studying that was ahead of him. She told him about her dream of being a music teacher, but how she really thought she would have to just do normal teaching, as her dad thought that doing music at university level was a waste of time and would probably lead to her listening to too much worldly music.

'I get his point,' she'd said, 'but I love music so much I would love to focus on it.'

He had agreed that she should do music if she wanted to, which she appreciated him saying.

Now she was preparing for the meeting, doing her usual bun shake, wanting it to be really nice so that he would appreciate her even more. She went down to the car, wearing her favourite dress, and smiled at him as she sat beside him. They had to go three miles down the road to the meeting, an unusual experience for Ella as she had grown up with the meeting in their home. It was at Grace and Hannah's house, too, so when she stayed there, they also didn't have to travel to the meeting.

Thankfully, the meeting felt like it flew by. Ella was finding it harder to sit in the meetings at the moment for some reason, even finding that she was wanting an excuse to not be in them. She felt shame about this, which made her pray harder in the mornings and evenings. Often they were told to appreciate every opportunity to be in a meeting, but she was going through a phase at the moment. She prayed regularly to be helped through it, but was getting impatient waiting for the Lord to answer her prayers. She didn't like the feeling.

As they all sat at the table and sang grace, Ella felt a renewed thankfulness for everything. After grace, she made small talk with David's mum, who seemed really nice. Perplexingly, though, every time Ella finished a conversation with her, she felt really confused about what had just happened.

'This is so tasty, Fiona, thank you!'

'Not a problem at all, Ella, what was it you were looking to study again? Music, was it?'

Ella hadn't told her this, so she presumed David had.

'Yeah! I just really love music.'

'Ah, I see, well make sure your job isn't something you love too much – you know you have to love God above all else.' Fiona said, staring unblinkingly at Ella.

'Of course I do, and I wouldn't let it get in between me and God, but I just really like it.'

'Yeah, I get that, of course – I felt the same about primary school teaching, but I never loved it. I also put my marriage and kids first. You know we are meant to really have that as our main purpose. I think people of your generation are really forgetting that. Don't get me wrong, I think it's good to get an education, but you should really stop when you get married.'

Ella smiled, slightly confused about how that had come up. She hadn't said anything about her beliefs on that, nor had she asked Fiona about it, but she let it pass without comment.

'I really like your dress – it's not something I would wear myself just because it's so short, but it is nice!'

'Oh thanks, I got it at Cents! Just ten euros. I know it's slightly short, but it's okay when I'm sitting down so I went for it anyway.'

Their conversation went on for the whole meal, after which Ella went for a walk with David.

'Your mum seems nice.'

'Yeah, she's the most important person in my life. I tell her everything.'

Ella nodded. Even though she felt slightly worse about herself after that short conversation. After all, Fiona had welcomed Ella into their house with open arms, which Ella appreciated. They made their way through the forest that was beside David's parents' land. They were walking through the trees, chatting about future plans, when David suddenly grabbed Ella's hand.

'Shh …'

'What's up?' Ella was happily surprised when she saw a couple of deer in front of them, grazing peacefully.

'Cute!'

'Yeah, they are pests, but they're also pretty cute to be fair.' David nodded. He turned towards Ella and took her other hand in his gently, leaning down towards her.

In response, she stood on her tippy toes and met his lips with her own. Her heart hammered in her chest as she focused on the kiss with all her might, trying to remember what she had read on the internet about kissing. She opened her lips slightly as his tongue gently pushed against them. It felt more clinical than she had imagined as she was focused so hard on doing it right that she couldn't really focus on the kiss itself.

They broke apart, both of them giggling self-consciously. David cleared his throat and let go of one of her hands wordlessly as they started walking further. After a bit, they stopped again and kissed some more. Ella enjoyed this one more, as she didn't have to concentrate as hard on the individual steps to kissing. He tasted of gravy and smelled slightly of pigs. Not the most attractive smell, but it suited him.

They kissed for a while longer and his hand started along her back, creeping lower. Ella wasn't sure if she was okay with that. While she had imagined kissing David plenty, she hadn't thought about how far she wanted to go with him, so she drew back.

'Are you okay?' he looked concerned.

'Yeah, I'm just not sure … about how far we should go?'

'Ah okay, well, we can figure that out together. You are very cute, though.' He winked and she blushed.

'You're cute too.' She felt slightly awkward saying it, but she did mean it. She normally only told those things to her friends, so it felt weird saying it to the guy himself.

When Ella went back home, she was buzzing with happiness about the weekend. She called Hannah, who was back in Ireland again and they agreed to meet up. Then she called Grace and they talked about the weekend. Grace was very excited for her, wanting as many details as possible. When Ella was finished explaining the whole weekend to the minute, Grace told her about her own brewing romance with one of the guys close to where she lived.

'I think he might be the one!' she said happily to Ella, who squealed.

Ella was out on a walk in their local park and attracted a few curious looks from passers-by, which she ignored.

'Really? Me too!'

'Imagine us both being married in a couple of years!' Ella said, jumping up and down.

'We can both have kids at the same time!'

'They can grow up together!'

'Of course, you'll have to move closer to us.'

'Or you could move closer to us, hello. Oh, but wait, David probably won't want to leave his parents' farm. And he'll be busy the next few years studying, we both will be.'

'Maybe we can both move to the wee north,' Grace said, mimicking David's strong accent.

'Oh aye, that would be great.'

'Your accent is terrible. Sorry to break it to you, love.'

'Hey! Take that back! I could definitely fit in up there.'

They teased each other for a while before hanging up. Ella was smiling. There was no one like Grace to keep you cheerful.

Adrian had gone to the meeting that Sunday morning. He was feeling so guilty – his mum had called him to make sure that he was going that morning. He read his Bible a minute before going in, finding a random verse that didn't offend him too much and went in. The whole meeting, he felt awful about his actions the night before, but knew he would do it again in a heartbeat. That thought only made him feel more guilty about it. The singing hurt his head, but he tried to act normally. No one said anything to him after the meeting, barely acknowledging his presence, so he didn't know if they could read his mind or if they genuinely didn't like him. It was weird – he normally had overall good experiences with the friends, with a few odd things that put him off. This meeting, however, was so cold towards him that he knew he wouldn't be coming back. That evening, with Harry lying across his lap, he wrote out a message.

'Hi Thomas, I will not be returning to the meeting. Regards, Adrian.'

He hit send and went back to watching the TV in Harry's living room.

Ella heard that Adrian had stopped going to meetings a week later. She cried about it with her mum, both of them fearing for his eternal life.

'I just hope he someday realises that more freedom isn't the freedom it seems; I hope he realises that you get more freedom within the way,' was all her mum had said about it. Ella's heart broke a little. Her heart broke even more later that evening when she got a different text.

'Hi, Ella, I'm sorry to say this in a text, but I have had no peace since last weekend. I believe that God wants us to split up. I really liked you. David.'

She stared at the message and put her phone down. Too much. She walked across the room, turned around, walked back, and broke down crying. She didn't understand it; it was so random. She had felt perfectly fine about the relationship and hadn't thought that she had lost any peace. Did that mean that she wasn't in good enough contact with God? Why did David get the answer? Why didn't she?

She recovered from the shock within a day, but she still felt horrible about the experience. When she met up with Hannah that weekend, she hadn't told her that he had broken up with her – she hadn't known how to, but when she and Hannah started talking, she couldn't help but break down crying about it.

'I just don't understand how he could do it like that – I thought we were getting on really well,' she sobbed.

'It's really mean of him to do that,' Hannah said, rubbing Ella's back in consolation.

When she had calmed her breathing down a little, Ella sighed.

'Am I ever going to find someone who is going to like me and it will be meant to be? What if all the men I ever date get told the same thing by God or go in the work? I don't want to get in the way of God's plan, but I also want to end up with someone at some stage.'

Hannah looked down at her feet. 'I worry the same thing, too. They spoke about it at convention this year, remember? That worker had been dating that woman for *five years* and they broke up! Just imagine how heart-breaking that would be. Although of course God would help you get through it, as He never puts us through more than we can manage, it's still so hard.'

Ella felt slightly reassured that she wasn't the only person who was feeling this way, but she was still worried about it. She would have felt happier if Hannah had told her that she was wrong and that it wouldn't happen, but she appreciated her honesty.

'I know. I'm sorry for spoiling the mood so much –
you were going to tell me all about the trip? How was
Nigeria, was it amazing?'

Hannah frowned. 'Erm, it was and it wasn't. You
know, everyone who has been there and I've ever spoken
to has really enjoyed their experience in Nigeria and have
raved about the people there, but I saw so much poverty at
my grandparents' house. My mum's parents live on the
outskirts of Lagos city and in a pretty nice area – it's
different, but it was comfortable. My dad's parents, though
… Um … It's kind of like night and day. In Lagos, they
have a nice enough house, it's loud in the area, and it's
small but they own it, you know?'

Ella nodded.

'They have nice things, they can rely on their
electricity and water, my grandad is university educated,
Grandma isn't, but she is smart, she's so interesting to have
conversations with. My other grandparents, they live out
beside a small town called Ijari and there's no predictable
electricity, their house is kind of dirty – my grandmother
has struggled with her mental health all her life, I think,
and there's basically no care for her. Mum was telling me
that the last law they brought in in Nigeria to do with
mental health was called the Lunacy Act.'

'What?' Ella interjected.

'I know, right? I think even the name of it pretty
much sums up the care she has access to. I just feel so bad
for her – she is clearly struggling so much and the workers
can't even get her help. They can look after the other
workers but not the friends. My grandmother really needs
help urgently or she might end up committing suicide or

hurting someone else. Mum and Dad agree, but it is going to be expensive.' Hannah started crying and Ella felt horrible for making a big deal out of her two-minute relationship.

'That's really tough. Why do the workers not help her? As you said, any time the workers have problems with their own health at all, they generally get medicine from home or go home if it's that bad, and it kind of sounds like it is that bad.'

'Yeah, I kind of think that the attitudes of the normal people there, as well as a lot of the workers over there, is that mental health is something you can pray away. I asked Mandy about it – she was there with us – and she said, and I quote, "I agree, your grandmother is very ill, but if she prays harder about it, with God she can find a peace beyond all understanding." I didn't even know what to say to that. Also, she kept calling it a nerves problem when it's so clearly mental health?' Hannah took a deep breath and then a gulp of her water when she finished speaking.

'I don't even know what to say about that. Were any of them being reasonable about it? I always liked Mandy, I'm kind of surprised to hear that from her …'

'Yeah, I was too. Actually, Kristina was the most reasonable about the whole thing – she was agreeing that we needed to get Granny to get help.' Hannah took a few deep breaths. It was clear that the experience had tarnished her perspective of the trip. 'I guess I always knew she wasn't that well, Mum would have told me about it, but Dad never spoke about his mum – I think he was kind of ashamed of her or something. I mean, culturally it makes sense; they don't talk about it much in Nigeria to be honest.'

They stayed for five hours talking in the café, and by the end of it both girls had settled down and felt comforted. When they left to go their separate ways, they hugged and Ella walked to the bus station, messaging her mum to let her know the approximate time the bus would be arriving. She couldn't wait until she could start driving herself. Waiting for other people to pick her up plus the irregular bus times was quite irritating. It also meant she spent a lot of her life waiting for things any time she went somewhere without her parents.

As she sat in the bus station, she heard a voice that sounded familiar and glanced up. Her own granny was standing just in front of her, staring at the timetable and talking to the man at the desk, asking him when the next bus was leaving.

'The next bus to Greenwelsh will be leaving in three hours, okay?'

'Ah, I see, why is that?'

'There's a bit of traffic going on with the football match at the moment.'

'Oh yeah, I forgot about that.'

'Granny!'

'Oh, Ella! I didn't expect to see you here?' Her grandmother turned and walked over to her, smiling. Ella stood up and they hugged.

'Yeah, I was just in town visiting Hannah. She's just back from Nigeria, you know?'

'Oh yes, I heard that she was going over there. Did she have a good time?'

'I think so … Mostly good, yes.' Ella didn't want to say too much to her grandmother, as she wasn't professing. Ella had learned from her mother that it was best to keep things like that kind of quiet from her granny. This was mostly so she wouldn't put her off the idea of ever coming back to meetings. Anna had explained, when Ella asked, that while they weren't a perfect people, they were in a perfect way. So, while the people would occasionally make mistakes, the way itself was worth it. She remembered that they had been told the evening before that they were happier when they didn't ask questions about things. While Ella didn't find everything the workers did 'perfect', she had stopped trying to ask questions internally about it. She was finding she was happier for it.

'Was everything okay?'

Ella started a little as she had kind of got lost in her own thoughts.

'Yeah … sure. I mean, yeah of course,' she corrected. 'How are you, Granny?'

'I'm good, Ella. Sure, you know yourself, I'm not getting any younger and I'm in a bit of pain every so often, but I think that is all part of getting older.'

Ella took her grandmother in for a few moments, considering what she had said.

'Are you okay? Where are you hurting?'

'Well, I've been having a few twinges in my side recently, and I haven't really had much of an appetite lately but I'm sure it'll sort itself out.'

Ella looked at her granny with some concern.

'Have you been to the doctor with that? That sounds kind of serious.'

'Oh, I suspect it'll all be fine. I'm just an old woman complaining,' she said and winked.

'Okay, Granny, but maybe you should go anyway, just to make sure? Would you do that for me?'

'Okay, if you say so, dear, but I think you are worrying about nothing, just like your mother,' she said, affectionately.

'Yeah … hopefully.'

'Anyway, I heard you are hoping to be a music teacher? Isn't that exciting?'

'Well, yeah … I mean, I would like to be a music teacher, but they were saying it might be too worldly – I'll have to listen to a lot of worldly music and one of the workers, Fred—'

Her grandmother clamped her hand to her mouth and Ella stopped speaking.

Ella stared, confused, then continued, 'He said that I should go for a career more suited to a professing woman.'

Her granny took a deep breath, straightened the hem of her skirt, and looked down for a second or two. She seemed to be stalling for time to think before she answered.

'I wouldn't worry too much about what that worker thinks, Ella. If I were you, I would just choose my own career path. After all, they aren't the ones who will have to go to work every day – they aren't going to do it for you.'

Ella nodded and made noises of assent, but she privately thought she wouldn't take any advice from the person who had ended up outside the meetings. She obviously didn't know enough to stay in, so how could she know enough to advise Ella on a path that would keep her on the way? She did want to believe her granny, but she tried not to think about it too much at the moment. They continued talking, with Ella asking after her grandad. After a while, Ella noticed that her bus had still not come, so she went over to the desk.

'Hi, I was just wondering if bus 45 is coming? I thought it was meant to be leaving now?'

'Yeah the bus 45 is delayed three hours. Our apologies for the inconvenience.'

Ella thanked the lady at the desk, who was looking very tired, and went and reported the news to her grandmother.

'Oh, mine is delayed until then – they said there's a GAA match today.'

'Ah right, I didn't even know, I don't pay any attention to Gaelic football. Maybe I should a bit more so I don't get caught out by their matches so often.'

Her granny nodded, then asked, 'Do you want to come with me and we'll get something to eat? My treat, I'm sure you're starving.'

Ella was. It was five-thirty and she was starting to feel her stomach make a protest about it. She had eaten at the café, but that had been at twelve and she had only eaten soup. She had thought she would be home by now or at the very least on the way. She agreed and sent her mother a message to make sure she wouldn't be waiting at the bus stop for her. Then she followed her granny to a restaurant down the road. There was only one table left, which they took.

'I really like this restaurant,' her granny confessed.

'Do you come here a lot?' Ella asked, glancing around, noticing a pair of ornamental dogs on the dark wooden mantelpiece above the open fireplace, which had a painting inside of it instead of a fire.

'Yeah. When I'm in town I tend to come here for a visit. My old school friend owns this restaurant, so I come here to catch up with her.'

'Ah okay! Very nice!'

They sat down. Her grandmother's face lit up and Ella turned around to see a lady who looked about twenty years older than her grandmother hobble across the room and give her grandmother a hug. She didn't understand how she looked so much older than her granny.

'This is Ella, my granddaughter.'

'Ah, Ella! I've heard so much about you!'

Ella couldn't say the same about this lady, so she just smiled at her. 'Nice to meet you.'

'What can I get for you lovelies? I would come over and chat as we normally do, Flo, but we're just a bit busy at the moment, short staffed, you know how it is.'

Ella's granny nodded. 'Of course, don't you worry about that at all, we'll be grand.'

When they'd ordered, Florence turned her attention back to her granddaughter.

'So, I heard from your mum that you went up to visit a nice young man?'

'Yeah, it didn't really work out, though,' Ella said, slightly awkwardly.

'Aw, that's a shame, why not?'

'Well …' She didn't know how her grandmother would react to being told that he had broken up with her because he had lost his peace about it. Her granny looked so open and welcoming, though, so Ella went ahead and told her, if just to avoid the awkwardness.

'Ah, so they are still using that reason.' Florence looked reflective as Ella glanced up at her in surprise.

'Someone broke up with you because of that?'

'Oh yes, I think two different guys did actually. It was their easy way out. Sorry you've been through that, Ella.'

Ella didn't know what to think. Was it because her granny wasn't professing anymore that she was saying this, that she had lost out, or was it true? Ella was confused about this. She kind of agreed with her granny, though.

Florence saw her granddaughter's thoughtful face and must have guessed what she was thinking.

'I originally thought the first guy had a good point, but when the second guy did it, I didn't believe him at all. It's the professing person's easy way out of a relationship without having to give you an actual reason. What was his mum like?'

'She seemed nice.'

'Did you always feel funny about yourself after talking to her, though?'

'Yeah.' Once again, Ella was surprised about her grandmother's insight.

'Yeah, I'd say it might be his mum's fault. I don't know her, of course, she may be lovely, but that is the pattern I've seen before. Pick yourself up, Ella. You'll get through this and find a young lad who will appreciate you for all that you are.' Florence was being careful with how she worded things around her granddaughter. She knew the

wrong wording could get her to sink in behind that familiar
block and her eyes would become slightly glazed over.
That was a sign that she was only seeming to listen, but
wasn't really taking it in.

They continued talking about more neutral topics,
such as hobbies, her grandmother's own childhood hobbies
and the pets Anna and her siblings had had when they were
young. When they went back to the bus station to catch
their buses, Ella felt a tug of sadness about leaving her
grandmother. She seemed like such an interesting woman
and really open. She wished she could spend more time
with her. She hoped her grandmother would profess, as it
would mean that they could have a much closer
relationship. They hugged as they said goodbye.

'It has been really nice to get to know you, Ella.'

'Yeah, I've really enjoyed this, Granny, thank you
for lunch! We should do this again sometime!'

'Definitely. Love you, Ella'.

'Love you too!' They walked onto their respective
buses and waved at each other through the window as first
Florence's bus and then Ella's made their separate ways
out onto the road.

Ella settled into her book, smiling slightly to
herself.

Chapter Twelve

Ella sat in the sun, enjoying the last bits of sunshine while waiting for her friends to join her. It was the end of September, and the weather was giving the Irish a last reminder of what it could do before the usual rain of the autumn. Ella was settling into the routine of school, homework, piano and flute lessons, alongside the gospel meetings three times a week.

Her friends, Niamh and Grainne, walked over to her, carrying their lunches.

'Hey, Ella, how was your morning?' Niamh, with her purple streaks through a mane of black hair, had a heart of gold, but the teachers hated her. She was always pushing the boundaries.

'Ah now, it was okay. Mrs O'Driscoll was her usual fun self, but otherwise it was alright. How were your mornings?'

'Grand,' Niamh replied, unwrapping her sandwich carefully and setting her napkin on her lap.

Grainne sighed and started into her sandwich, pushing her braid behind her back.

'Shit. I think I'll quit. Start up a business selling sweets or something. I'm already well on my way to becoming a successful businesswoman. It's good for our gender, or whatever the hell that prick was on about the other day.'

Niamh laughed.

'He was saying we can do whatever we want. You know, it's a modern world out there. We can do whatever we want and be whoever we want to be.'

'Why the hell was it a man anyway? We're in an all-girls' school, full of female teachers. I don't understand why a man had to give the speech.'

'My dad still won't let me be a music teacher, so what does it matter?' Ella said with a shrug.

'My dear, that was the whole fucking point of the fucking speech. Who cares what the hell your dad thinks?'

'I mean, it's not just my dad.'

'What do you mean? Surely it's not that bad to be a music teacher? Like, where is the line – would he be happy if you were going to be a doctor, or a lawyer or something?'

'Being a doctor would probably be okay. I don't know about a lawyer.'

'Why the fuck does it matter?'

'It's because of my religion …' Ella felt uncomfortable. She never talked about this stuff with her friends. She tried to keep it separate.

'Yeah, okay, but what is your religion?' Niamh asked gently.

'It doesn't have a name.' Ella's heart sped up. Her least favourite question.

'Ya okay, you've told us that before, but what is it? Like why all the secrecy?'

'I'm not being secretive, it literally doesn't have a name.' Ella's words came out weaker than she wanted, so she cleared her throat.

'So, you all meet in a home and those random fuckers, what are they called again?'

'Workers. Please don't call them that, Grainne.'

'Oh sorry, force of habit. So those random workers, they stay in your house, right?'

'Yeah.'

'Is that not super creepy? Like they just stay overnight, in your house. Don't they have their own houses to stay in?'

'No, they leave home and all their belongings behind.'

'Okay, so they leave their parents or whoever, and then they what? How do they leave their houses without any belongings?'

'They just go …' Ella shifted on the bench. She liked her friends a lot, and knew they were good people. She also knew that this was a chance for her to show her friends what they were missing out on. Maybe someday they would even profess and go to the conventions and meetings and missions with her. Although Grainne was an atheist, and Niamh was a devout Catholic. But still, you never knew. God works in mysterious ways.

'Okay, and why do they think that you shouldn't be a music teacher?'

Because Dad thinks I'll be listening to too much worldly music, Ella thought.

'They just don't think it's appropriate, I don't know.'

They left it there and moved on to gossiping about the guys from the all-boys school across the town, some of whom came over to their school after dinner. Ella secretly thought that one of them was quite cute but didn't admit it to anyone. He wasn't one of the friends, so she shouldn't have a relationship with him – she knew that. Either way, she was incredibly glad to not have to talk about her beliefs anymore. She wasn't good at coming up with answers to their questions. One time, Grainne had got into a whole argument with one of the boys from the all-boys' school, Oisín, who was also a devout Catholic, and Oisín had asked for her support.

'You're religious, aren't you?' he'd asked.

'Yeah, I suppose I am,' she'd replied.

'Dude, she is super fucking religious!' Had been Grainne's input.

Ella had taken offense at that but said nothing. The religious people were those in the churches, she knew. But even though she knew better, she wouldn't argue about it.

He had asked her to side with him, to help support some of his arguments, but she had found it hard to. It was easy with the friends – they knew what one another meant, but with worldly people, like school friends, it was harder. She would have to explain the whole thing, and then they would bring up arguments towards it, which wouldn't matter. But because Ella wasn't good at arguing or debating, she would just have to leave it, knowing that she knew the right way, the only way that would allow her to get into heaven. They had also gone into some details that she just didn't know the answer to, and Grainne had come up with some pretty detailed arguments. Ella just felt sad for her friend, who was so clearly influenced by the devil and the world. She had brought the conversation up at dinner that evening and her dad had been able to explain everything away, and told her not to listen to those friends again and their negative influence.

'I know they are your friends, Ella, but they are still of the world and of our enemy, especially those atheists. They are sent to test you, but we have to be true to the Lord, and He will help us safely through all of these experiences. If we stay close to Jesus and to God, we are more equipped to take on the world. Make sure that you stay close to them, Ella.'

Ella felt chastened, but also reassured. Her friends weren't right, after all; she just had to pray more to God. She did so that night, but also never brought anything like it up with her father again, because she felt so embarrassed about being close to the devil. He for his part never mentioned it again either. It was like that with her parents – they would punish or tell you off for something once, but after that it was never brought up again. They forgave very easily.

Ella sighed deeply as she turned another page of her book. She was on holiday at last, and while she still had some work to do for school – whatever idiot came up with that idea, she would dearly like to have a word with – she was taking some time to fully relax and enjoy the season. It was Christmas Eve, and tomorrow the Christmas meetings were meant to start. After tomorrow's meetings, they would have a family dinner with her dad's side of the family, then on the thirtieth with her mum's side of the family. The fire was crackling, and the country was experiencing one of the biggest snowfalls ever. They weren't even sure if they would be able to have the get-together tomorrow, or even the special meeting, but Ella didn't care at this moment in time. Finally, a white Christmas for the first time in her lifetime.

The candles in the corners of the room and on the table burned brightly, creating a cosy effect, and the smell of cinnamon and nutmeg filled the room. Ella sipped at her tea, took another bite of her gingerbread cookie, and continued to read. It was an easy read, a break from her Irish and English reading, which often included complicated language and took a lot of concentration to get through. She was fully immersed in the lives of the characters, wanting the two main characters to get together.

She glanced up as a snowman walked into the room.

'Hey, Ella,' said the snowman cheerfully, brushing away some of the snow to reveal Adrian.

'Oh, hi, Adrian!' Ella hadn't seen her brother since they had moved all of his things to his room in Dublin. She uncurled herself, gently moved her cookie and tea out of the way as she had absentmindedly placed them on the footstool in front of her, and stood up to hug her brother. They hugged and Ella forced a small tear away from the corner of her eye with the palm of her hand. She had missed her brother more than she would let on, even to herself.

Adrian's shoulders released. His cheery façade had been a huge amount of effort on his part. He was very nervous about how he would be received. He of course still had to see his parents, but at least Ella seemed to be outwardly okay with his presence. He had been in touch with his mother, of course – she checked in on him regularly and had been down to visit a couple of times. Each announcement of her intention to visit had prompted a warning to the housemates to not mention his exact relationship with Harry and a rapid tidy-up of their house. His housemates weren't completely untidy, but they did drink a lot more than Anna would approve of. Adrian himself had started the term by drinking heavily nearly every night for a week, in an attempt to get rid of some feelings that he didn't want to face. Thankfully, Harry had pointed out to him that this was an unhealthy way of coping and also very expensive, so now he only drank more than a beer in the evening every few weeks. Adrian had also tried weed, which had made him sick, joined the chess club, which was terrible, then resorted to watching TV and playing video games for the next while, only surfacing to do something with Harry or to go to lectures. He had made no friends and was now relying on Harry as his only form of socialising.

On Harry's part, he had adapted pretty well, having seen the college counsellor, and was feeling better for it. He had made friends with people in his swimming club and they socialised together. Adrian was kind of jealous. They weren't really officially dating. They were in this strange in-between phase where they hung out a lot and kissed sometimes, even letting it go further on a few occasions. It was messy and Adrian hated mess, especially when it involved a lifelong friend. He knew that Harry deserved more in a relationship, but he couldn't provide it, nor did he want to let him go. He knew it wasn't completely fair to Harry, but it was just hard and complicated and another thing that Adrian felt bad about, alongside not going to the meetings anymore and being bisexual in the first place.

Their friendship was holding them together, but it still felt like it was falling apart at the seams. He pushed these worrying thoughts aside, as he so often did and focused on his sister. Something felt off as the pair chatted and teased each other in the unique manner only siblings can. They had lost a connection that had been there even though he had become more closed off the last year.

'I heard you ended up in hospital?' Ella frowned at her brother.

'Yeah, I had severe stomach pain again, but it's all good now.'

'Did they find the cause?'

'No, none of the tests showed anything in particular, but it went away itself, thankfully. Guess my body is just kind of weird.' Adrian laughed and Ella joined in.

'Yeah, I suppose so, but sure it's good that nothing showed up.'

Adrian was teasing Ella about a boy at their local mission when the rest of the family walked in. They had been attempting a walk in the snow, but it hadn't gone entirely to plan, resulting in his parents, covered in snow and a rather bedraggled looking, slightly lanky snowman walking in. Justin had shot up since Adrian had last seen him. They dripped over the carpet, and Anna asked Ella to grab some towels for them. Ella did so, and as she was walking away, she heard Anna exclaim, 'Adrian!' and Adrian's protests to Justin, who had apparently decided it would be the perfect time to hug him. She smiled as she reached for the towels, accidentally toppling half the pile on top of herself, which she quickly replaced as she heard Anna scolding about the soaking floor. As Ella walked back, Adrian, with a Justin-shaped wet mark on his clothes, was walking towards the cupboard, looking genuinely happy. He fetched the mop at his mother's orders, grinned widely at Ella, and the two of them walked back into the chaos.

That evening, as they all sat around the table, the energy was high. Anna brought out the food and they all sat quietly. Peter looked at Anna, who looked back at him.

'Would you start, Ella?' They sang grace, as with every meal, and Adrian, who had momentarily forgotten and already taken a bite, felt a strange tug of nostalgia at this custom. It had taken him a while to stop pausing before every meal, even though he had originally tried to say thanks for every meal, he didn't feel like it after a while. He felt an emptiness when he tried to do anything to communicate with God. He had never really felt a connection, but what little connection he had had seemed to be completely gone.

They never mentioned the fact that Adrian had stopped going to the meetings, he observed. They made regular mentions of the workers and what they were doing however, and discussed who was coming out to the meetings, who had recently professed, who was visiting for the special meetings. It felt a little bit like meetings were the only topic of conversation they wanted to cover, but Adrian couldn't complain. He was with his family, and he felt loved. He had felt quite lonely the last while and would take all of the meeting talk just to feel the company around him. After everything was cleared up, Anna looked with some concern at the clock.

'I thought Marjorie and Anna would be back by now …'

'Are Marjorie and Anna staying?'

'Yes, just for a couple of nights. You'll be sleeping in the living room if that's okay?'

Adrian nodded, but he was feeling slightly blindsided. All of his warm feelings about being at home had sunk and he couldn't help but think that this was just typical. He knew he wasn't living at home anymore, but this had happened so often in his life. He was fed up with having to move all of his belongings out of his room every time two workers wanted to stay at the same time. Sometimes he would stay with Justin, but he suspected his parents didn't want their black sheep influencing the innocent mind of their good, well-behaved children. His stomach hurt again.

'Where are they gone to? That weather is awful for them to be driving back in.' Maybe they would have to stay there for the night.

'Oh, just to the O'Learys.' The O'Learys lived two minutes down the road so even if they couldn't drive, they would probably just walk it. Damnit. He excused himself to go upstairs to the bathroom, where he threw up. He was stuck here now, in a home that stressed him out, possibly for quite a while, as that weather was really terrible out there. He heard someone come up the stairs. They knocked.

'Who is it? I'm in here.'

'Hey, are you okay?' It was Justin.

Adrian was surprised.

'Yeah, I'm fine. Thanks …'

'Do you think it was the chicken?'

'Yeah, that's probably it.' Justin was being more empathetic than Adrian remembered him being. It was weird to him to think of his brother growing up while he wasn't there to see it.

'So … how have you been?' Adrian asked from the inside of the toilet bowl.

'Good, mostly. I miss you – Ella doesn't ever want to play video games like we used to.'

Adrian smiled despite himself.

'I bet she doesn't. Hey, when I'm feeling a bit better, I'll play something with you, whatever you want, to make up for that, okay, bro?'

'Deal.' Justin paused. 'I don't think there'll be special meetings tomorrow.'

'Really?'

'Yeah, it'll give us more time to play games, right?'

'It will.'

So many Christmas Days given up to special meetings, Adrian thought. They tended to place the special meetings on Christmas Day as much as possible. He had had maybe four Christmas Days without special meetings in his life. They took up so much of the day. They would have to leave at eight-thirty in the morning, and would eat sandwiches for their Christmas dinner in the car. Then they would go back for the second two-hour meeting, before all going home at four pm or to a relative's house to eat Christmas dinner. They were at least better than Union meetings, which in Ireland happened every couple of months and included a random assortment of people from the local meetings, with generally one worker. They tended to last forever, and the rooms you were in were generally small with barely enough room for the number of people squeezed into it. One to his memory had even lasted for three hours on one particularly awful Sunday. No one had been happy about that, apart from the worker who had caused the problem by deciding to speak for an hour at the end.

When Adrian went back downstairs, three shapes were standing in the door, and there was a lively conversation happening. He stood at the doorway and squinted slightly, not recognising the tall shape. He took a few extra deep breaths and walked into the living room.

'And this is Adrian.' Anna pointed to him as he strolled across to the group, taking in the tall stranger and Ella's gaze at the tall guy. He pulled his fingers through his long black hair, then stepped forward to shake Adrian's hand and Adrian understood the gaze. He was exactly Ella's type. She would never admit it, but her real type was indie boys. She had gone out with that loser for a few minutes, with his tidy hair and his dealer boots, but every crush she had had that had lasted had been the summation of this man in front of her. He smiled to himself, knowing he could get plenty of mileage out of this topic later, and joined the conversation about how weird the weather was these days.

Chapter Thirteen

Christmas morning arrived with more snowstorms and news of the roads being shut all over the country. The brother workers had called Peter the evening before to announce that, for the first time in a long time, they would have to cancel the special meetings for the day. Ella didn't know what to think. She was shocked to find she was secretly delighted, an emotion she'd never imagined she'd have if the meetings were cancelled. It might or might not have had everything to do with the attractive man who had walked into her house and into her mind the night before. It felt like every thought she was now having was revolving around *him*.

With previous crushes, and even the short-term relationship she'd had with David, she had never been so instantly enamoured with someone. Not that she was in love with him, of course – that would be ridiculous. He just oozed confidence from every pore. He even had long hair, which was unusual for a professing guy. It barely reached his shoulders, but still. His style wasn't the typical Irish guy style, with a pair of jeans and dealer boots, but he wore his chinos and open green linen shirt layered with a T-shirt like the clothes had been made specifically for him. Last night, when he had shaken the snow off himself, and removed the thick jacket, jumper and boots, revealing a carefully sculpted set of arms and shoulders, Ella hadn't been able to breathe for a short while.

Now he was lying in the room next to hers. At least, she presumed he was; she hadn't heard a peep from him this morning yet and Ella knew that the wall was not very thick. She put some mousse in her hair to try and control it a little – she had learnt a hair tactic from one of the friends. It had turned her hair from a frizzy mess into a manageable, actually pretty mane that behaved mostly as she wanted it to, unless she went anywhere with water or humidity. Her braces had been removed that summer and she had suddenly started getting a lot more attention from the boys her age. She even sometimes had half a second's thought that she might be pretty, although she pushed the vain thoughts out of her head pretty quickly. Overall, though, she was feeling slightly more confident in her abilities to catch Ryley's attention.

They opened their Christmas presents together. The workers had taken forever to get up, something that Justin vocally protested against, until his parents told him to shut up and be glad that the workers were willing to stay with them that day. While they were waiting, Ryley arrived, and Ella wondered whether her mum had arranged a present for him.

'So how did you end up here anyway?' she asked.

'That's a long story,' Ryley laughed, and Ella joined in, gaining her a look and a wink from Adrian. She stopped abruptly and blushed.

'You're American, right?' Justin, sitting in the corner, reading, joined in.

'No, I'm Canadian.'

'Justin, you should know that.'

'How would I know that? They all sound the same.'

'Dude, that is literally like me calling you English and saying you sound the same,' Ella said, thankful that she hadn't asked to guess because that had been her assumption, too.

'Yeah, pretty much.'

'So, how did you end up here?' Justin asked.

'It's a long story, as I said. The short version is that I am travelling this year before I start university. I was first travelling around Europe, then I ran out of money when I arrived in Ireland. I am going to start working for the O'Learys on their farm, but I was invited to your place by your mom when she called them and heard I was staying here. I also have an Irish passport, so I can stay here long term, whereas I had to leave the likes of Spain and Greece after a while.'

'You didn't want to stay with the O'Learys for Christmas?' Adrian chuckled to himself even as he asked it. The O'Learys, while a nice enough couple, weren't exactly who you would want to spend your holiday with.

'No, they didn't really want me there either, I don't think, and they had enough help until the twenty-seventh, so I was just eating their food, according to Harriet.'

The three in the know exchanged glances. That sounded accurate, Ella thought.

'Well, you're very welcome here,' Ella said and smiled.

The workers came downstairs soon after, so she didn't get much of a chance to learn more about him. They opened the presents, sat in a circle, and just soaked up the moments. Ella kept stealing glances at Ryley's profile. After the presents had been enjoyed (her mum had got

something for Ryley, after all) and they had made a start
with the sweets and chocolates that were in the stockings,
they put on their warm clothes and made the most of the
snow.

The old, battered sleigh was dragged out of the
shed, and they had the best time going down the hill at the
back of their house. The younger sister worker even joined
in, borrowing a pair of leggings from Ella. A snowman
contest was held, with Peter as the judge and Ryley
winning. Then they had a snowball fight with everyone
yelling as it descended into chaos. When they came back
inside, dripping wet, they were welcomed with hot
chocolate prepared by Anna. Adrian felt significantly better
about everything for just a few moments. He glanced at
Ella, who was glowing as she chatted away with Ryley. It
was cute. His stomach had stopped hurting him so much,
he noticed. He was starting to suspect it had something to
do with anxiety.

Ella and Ryley had started talking when they'd
teamed up for the snowman contest. There had been an
ease to the conversation as they decided their approach,
which, according to Ryley, would be the winning factors.
Ella felt nervous talking to him, but also comfortable
somehow. By the time they arrived back at the house, she
had learned about his siblings. He went upstairs to get
photos of his two sisters and brother. He was the second,
with an older sister of twenty-one, then himself at eighteen,
another sister of sixteen, and a ten-year-old brother. Ella
sipped on her hot chocolate as she waited from Ryley to
fetch the album and saw Adrian approach her with a
twinkle in his eye.

'You like him!' he sang in her ear. She batted him away.

'Shut up, let me have my own life.' She stuck her tongue out at him. He poked her playfully, laughing as she blushed. Ryley walked back into the room, so she shoved Adrian away and tried to hide her red cheeks.

'So, this is us.' He showed her a printout of two girls wearing jeans and Ryley and another boy. Ella stared. Jeans?

'Are they all going to meetings?' She tried to hide the surprise in her voice.

'Oh yes, actually Sasha professed last year!'

'Ah okay, do girls wear jeans there?'

'Yeah, of course!'

'That is pretty different to here.' They walked over to the seats in the corner.

'Well, if you think about it, it doesn't say anything against it in the Bible, so in Vancouver you'll see quite a few of the young ones wearing jeans. Especially when we're doing something active together.'

They chatted for a while undisturbed as the others had their own conversations on the other side of the room and the workers went upstairs. Anna was checking the turkey, which she had originally bought for the day after, but had decided to cook today instead. The rest of the family wouldn't be coming tomorrow anyway the way the weather was at the moment. She called for help as the task of the vegetable and meat preparations started to overwhelm her.

Ella and Ryley got up to help her and spent more time chatting as they set the table and washed dishes, finding joy together in the mundane preparations for the Christmas dinner. Anna observing the pair, who were laughing together, while Justin and Adrian disappeared to play video games.

When the dinner was on the table, Ella and Ryley sat next to each other. Ella was used to pretending she didn't like boys, except with David, she had thought that she had to hide the fact that she liked them, but she felt comfortable being with Ryley and showing her interest in him in quiet ways.

When they had finished the 'best Christmas dinner ever', according to Justin, they sat and relaxed for a while. Once they had recovered, the younger ones, the worker included, went outside to make the most of the snow. And when they felt satisfied and frozen to their cores, they tumbled back inside, giggling about Justin's attempts to go sledging standing up. He hadn't succeeded, but the sight of his arms waving about as he fell dramatically had been hilarious.

As they were made to stand on the towel by the door by an Anna who considered having to dry the whole floor once *more* than enough, Ella felt Ryley's body very close to hers. She felt the heat come off it as he stood behind her, and she handed her coat to her mum, feeling embarrassed by her own feelings towards the man whom she was suddenly even more aware of. Watching her brother walk off the towel and sit down, she shook herself as she realised what she was doing. She forced herself to step further into the room.

They sat down, taking a rest as Peter suggested that they all play a few boardgames. The Uno was taken out and they all moved closer to the coffee table, with Ella ending up beside Ryley once again. Their arms brushed as they put their cards on the table. Justin won and was promptly accused of cheating by his two siblings. Ryley just sat back, observing the arguments with a slight grin.

'What are you smiling about?'

'I just missed this with my own brother and sisters.'

Ella nodded. 'I can imagine – how long is it since you saw them?'

'Six months now.'

'That is quite a while.'

'It is, yeah.' Ryley's eyes drifted towards the window as his eyes crinkled with a smile, lost in a memory Ella couldn't see.

It was already getting dark, and they were relaxing on the couch, when Ryley whispered to Ella, so as to not wake up Peter sleeping beside them, if she wanted to go for a walk with him. She nodded. They got their coats, scarves, gloves, and hats back on, and slipped out. They walked in silence, except for Ella suggesting that they go down the road the opposite way to the O'Learys. She pondered what this walk meant. They had been getting on really well so far, and he had even complimented her outfit and her hair, but she wasn't certain he was single. He was a bit too cute to be single, surely.

'Do you have a girlfriend?' she blurted out when she couldn't take it anymore.

'Not for a year or so. Do you have a boyfriend?'

'No, I don't.'

He nodded and they continued walking in silence, until he pointed to the stars. 'It's so clear tonight.'

'It is.' Ella couldn't take it anymore. She had only known this guy for twenty-four hours, but she wanted to kiss him for every minute of those twenty-four hours. She cleared her throat.

'Ryley?'

'Yeah?'

'When are you going to kiss me already?'

He laughed as he took her face in his hands. She could feel his breath.

'It's refreshing to hear a girl be so blunt about it.'

Her own breathing faltered as he lowered his face closer to hers, and she lifted her face to meet his lips, but they weren't there yet.

'Don't get me wrong …' His voice had deepened considerably. 'I want to kiss you real bad, but I need to tell you something first.'

He let her go and took a step back, both of them breathing rapidly.

'I know that we're expected to wait before marriage.'

Ella blinked. That wasn't what she had expected.

'I probably won't be able to. I don't think that sex before marriage is a true sin, no matter what the workers believe. It doesn't mean I want to have sex with you immediately, or any time soon, but I think it should be a part of a normal relationship.'

Ella didn't know what to say or think.

'I don't want to make you uncomfortable and would never ask you to do anything you aren't comfortable with. You can always say no in the moment – obviously consent is very important – but do you think you would be open to that? Be honest if it's a hard no – it's easier to break things off now than later I think.'

Ella stood there as her breathing returned to normal. Ryley stood back even further, as if trying to take himself out of the equation. She didn't know what to do.

'Can I just kiss you now and figure that out as we go along? My last boyfriend broke up with me after our first kiss, so maybe I kiss badly anyway and this isn't an important conversation?'

She didn't mean to give away her secret doubts like that, but she hadn't expected Ryley to say what he had either to be fair.

'Look, if it isn't a hard no, we can go ahead.'

'It's not a hard no,' she decided as she spoke.

He took a step closer to her. 'Are you sure?'

'Yes. For now.'

He nodded and took a step even closer to her, his fingertips on her chin, lifting it. She felt weak as his lips touched hers gently, and then more firmly. His other hand went under her arm, and she brought her hand to his waist, enjoying the smell of aftershave and fresh air off his skin as their kiss deepened. She felt his tongue teasing her lips as she opened them to let him in. As their tongues touched, a shiver ran through her. This was a kiss like she had read about in books. There were sparks bursting as he lifted her up. She wrapped her legs around him and suddenly understood why he said he couldn't wait. They kissed until they ran out of air, came up for air, and then kissed again. Butterflies and sparks and all kinds of twinkly things inhabited her body as they explored each other's mouths. Her hands ran through his hair, while his strong arms held her up. It started to snow as they hugged afterwards, enjoying each other's embrace.

They kissed so much on the way back to the house. Ella considered the difference afterwards, trying not to compare the two. She was, to her surprise, enjoying the fact that while he had been a lot more forthright than she was used to about sex, he had still not tried to cop a feel while they were kissing like David had. They slipped back into the house through the back door, giggling quietly and holding hands. They dropped their hands as they walked in, trying not to give their relationship away immediately. Once their coats and hats and gloves and scarves had been removed, they walked further inside. Adrian was standing in the hall, looking out at the snow when they passed him on the way to the kitchen.

'Where were you guys?' he asked, grinning.

'Oh, we just went for a walk,' Ryley replied, winking at Ella, who blushed.

Adrian tapped her on the arm as she followed Ryley into the living room. She turned.

'Hey, don't let him do anything you aren't comfortable with. If he tries anything or pushes you, call me and I'll beat him up for you, okay?'

'Okay, big guy,' she teased him, sticking her tongue out at her brother as she walked past.

Chapter Fourteen

The next day, when they all repeated the cycle of playing outside in the snow and coming inside to eat, fully embracing their inner child, they saw that they were clearing the road. Ella and Ry, as she now called him, were sneaking kisses behind everyone's backs. They had decided not to tell everyone yet and were enjoying the excitement that came with secrecy.

All too soon, Ryley had to go back down the road to the O'Learys' house for work starting at five am the next day. They said goodbye behind the house before he left after dinner. They would see each other the next day, as Ella was still off school until the New Year, so they agreed to meet up every day for a walk. Ryley would be able to drive the jeep belonging to the O'Learys, so they would be able to manage that, and he would have a couple of hours in the evenings. They still found it difficult to say goodbye, though. Ryley was nervous about starting work, as he hadn't really got on well with the couple yet, but Ella assured him that she was there for him and that they weren't really as scary as they'd seemed at first. The young couple exchanged a last long hug and parted, Ella disappearing inside to go up to her room to hug herself and do a happy dance.

Ella couldn't stop smiling. The more she thought about it, the more she started to appreciate how direct he had been. The thought of making love to him awoke feelings in herself that she had never experienced before.

She wondered what sex would be like. She had heard
things from her friends, but she had never really thought
about it in any detail before. It was wrong to have sex
before marriage, she knew that, but that was all she knew.
The workers never discussed the details, everything had
always been very vague. She sat down at her desk and
opened a drawer, reached into the drawer, and opened the
secret drawer. She pulled out the book that her school
friend Grainne had given her last year. Ella had shoved it in
there so her mum wouldn't take it off her like the last time
she had had a book like that. Trying to decide what to do,
she opened it up at that page she had come across again,
then she put it back and went back downstairs.

That night, after she was sure that her parents were
asleep, she took out the book again and read through the
first few pages. She knew about basic anatomy thanks to
her school friends, but her school itself had barely
mentioned sex. She read to the point where things started
to get heated before she stopped. But then she read the
words back, making sure she had understood properly.

'*He kissed the whole way down her naked body,
played with her nipple in his tongue, then went down
further, and further, to that point where all her nerves sat,
and teased her with his tongue.*' Surely he couldn't go into
her vagina with his tongue? Was there something else?

She shoved the book under her pillow when she
heard footsteps down the corridor, her heart and mind
racing. If someone in her family found out what she was
considering, she would properly be kicked out of her home.
She sat in silence as whoever it was went to the bathroom,

and didn't move until she heard them close the door of their bedroom.

She grabbed the book back out from under the pillow and went on reading.

'*His tongue went back and forth before she came to her sweet release. Then, looking deep into her eyes, he put his …*' Ella skimmed the word … '*inside her, filling her up.*'

So … there was something else? Her hand went down her underwear, wondering if she could find it. She found a sensitive point and moved her fingers over it, like the book said. She started to feel something build up and read on, moving her fingers faster and faster, until her whole body tensed up. Her tension suddenly released and an incredible feeling came over her. She lay back in her bed, wondering about it. She didn't have the words to comprehend what had happened, but she had enjoyed it. She felt an odd guilt about it, like she had done something wrong, but no one had ever told her that touching herself there was a sin, so she just tried to ignore those thoughts and went to sleep.

Ella went across the fields the next day after lunch to meet up with Ryley. She had got a good amount of work done, somehow managing to concentrate on something that wasn't Ryley. She texted him and they both walked halfway across the fields and met inside a shed that belonged to the O'Learys. It was Ryley's lunch break and he told her about his first day, which hadn't been as bad as he had imagined. It was mostly feeding stock and breaking ice off the drinkers at the moment, as the snow was putting all other work on hold and he wasn't needed in the milking parlour yet.

'So, you're free for the rest of the day essentially?'

'Yeah! I asked John and he said that I can come back to your house for the afternoon if your mom will let me?'

She kissed him in her excitement.

'My parents, Adrian, and Justin are going to the park,' she suddenly remembered. They were going to meet up with some of the friends for a walk in the snow now that the roads had been cleared.

'Oh, okay. Are you okay being home alone with me?' His eyes twinkled, but she appreciated him asking. They had only known each other a couple of days, after all.

'Yeah, of course, but I'm not ready to … you know … yet – is that okay?'

'Absolutely, I'm not ready for that yet either.'

Ella sighed a breath of relief.

'I'm not going to rush you into this, Ella, you can take as long as you need. The main point I feel strongly about is that no one should get married only for the purpose of being able to have sex. I saw that with someone I know, and it really didn't go well at all. I just figure that if we have that already, we are less likely to rush into something we don't necessarily want.'

'That makes sense.'

'I've also never had sex before – this is a newish revelation for me, just so you know that, too.'

Ella nodded. She was relieved.

'Let's go back to our house. I think they will already be gone.'

They walked back, hand in hand, talking about lighter subjects. They were still getting to know each other, and Ella was liking this boy the more she got to know about him. He was funny, but serious about the right things. They had the same sense of humour and both enjoyed a few of the same musicians. When they arrived back at the house, Ella was right. There was no one home. She called each name just to make sure and smiled shyly at Ryley.

'Do you want to see my room?'

'Are you sure?'

'Yep!'

She led him upstairs, pointing out different rooms as they made their way up the staircase. They stopped at the threshold of her room. She had tidied it just in case, just like she had shaved herself downstairs just in case. Her Bible and hymnbook sat perched on the side of her bedside table.

'Who are they?' Ryley walked over to her picture frame, full of photos of her with various friends and school friends.

'That's Hannah and Grace, my best friends. Hannah lives close by, but Grace lives at the convention grounds.'

'Ah okay! Cool.'

He turned around and walked over to Ella, who was standing at the side of her bed. He kissed her gently, lowering her onto the bed as he once again explored her mouth with his tongue. They lay side by side, just kissing. His hand rested on her waist, then started moving up and down her back, into her hair. It followed her hair which had fallen down the front. He stopped and pulled back.

'Would you be comfortable if I touched your boob?'

'Is your hand warm?' Ella giggled nervously.

'It is. Are you okay with that, though?'

She nodded. His fingers traced her jawline and then her collarbone, and then went down and he cupped her breast in his hand.

'You are beautiful.'

Ella's heart sped up. She wanted to argue with him, to tell him that he must have made a mistake – no one would find her beautiful. But, when her eyes met Ryley's, she saw sincerity there.

'Thanks.'

They continued kissing, just lying beside each other, gently exploring each other, but not going too far.

They spent the next few days following a similar pattern. Neither had to work too much because of the holidays, so they enjoyed spending time together quietly without anyone other than Adrian knowing. They told everyone else at New Year's Eve, just before other people arrived for the party as they wanted to share a New Year's kiss.

At the end of the week, after New Year's, Adrian left. He hadn't gone to the special meetings they had had, much to Ella's disappointment. Ella and Ryley hadn't gone any further but had met up with each other every day that week.

As Adrian was leaving the house, he gave Ella a hug. Ella, suddenly filled with a love for her brother. She didn't want to leave it as long before they saw each other again.

'Can we get a coffee sometime soon? Catch up?'

'Of course! We'll keep in touch, organise a date?'

Ella nodded and waved as he drove off, wondering how she was going to ask him the question that had been nagging at the back of her head for a while now.

Chapter Fifteen

Ella sat perched on the edge of her seat. Her hair wasn't wild for once and she was wearing a shorter skirt than usual – it only reached halfway down her knee. She had bought a hair straightener a couple of weeks ago and had used it. She was now feeling incredibly rebellious, looking around at regular intervals to make sure a worker or one of the friends didn't walk past. She was tapping her feet. She knew that people were often caught as they did things like this – the workers spoke of it often and her mother had told her of the time she had been caught buying a pair of hiking trousers by an older brother worker. It was the reason they always wore skirts on hikes if the workers were with them. They didn't wear them if the workers weren't with them, though – leggings were enough. Ella thought about what Ryley had said about his sisters just wearing jeans. It was still a hard thing for her to wrap her head around.

She spotted Adrian across the shopping centre and waved. He saw her and came over. She was suddenly aware of her new hairstyle. She hoped he wouldn't think she was on her way out or something, but she doubted he would even notice.

'Hey, Ella.'

'Adrian, hi!'

Adrian asked where she'd like to go for coffee, immediately complimenting her new hairstyle to her surprise. They settled on a small café that Adrian loved – he was getting to know the staff, as he came here quite a lot to study since it was becoming hard to study in his room. He was finding it difficult to keep his living space liveable, which had meant that he and Harry were only hanging out in Harry's place, as Adrian was embarrassed about how bad it was getting. He knew it would only take a few hours to clean it, but he wasn't able to face it right now.

The brother and sister started with small talk – the weather, school – before they moved onto Ella and Ryley's relationship, which was going well. What Ella didn't say was that she had let Ryley go further than she had ever considered. She felt like things might progress into new territory soon enough. She didn't have anyone to talk to about that other than Ryley himself, so she just pushed it down. It was embarrassing.

'Why did you leave?' Ella felt like her mouth had opened before she was ready.

'Leave home?'

'Well yeah, but mostly, why did you leave the meetings?'

He just looked at her. He hadn't been asked this yet and he had been out for a year and a half already.

Ella mistook his surprise for reluctance. 'Only if you want to tell me, of course …'

Adrian took a deep breath.

'I never really believed in everything the way you do. I never felt that it was the only way, or that we should really dedicate our whole lives to it the way everyone else does. I really only joined in because I knew it made our parents happy and I was kind of jealous of how they treated you when you professed.'

Ella was intrigued. She had known that their parents had treated her in a preferential manner on some level when she had professed that fateful evening, even compared to how Adrian had been treated. She had also seen that he never really loved it like she did, as he had often pushed the boundaries without seeming to worry too much. She had never said anything, though, nor dwelled on it too much. She had always hoped that he was just going through a phase, or that she was misreading the signs.

'So, last year, when something horrible happened to me which also reminded me of other things that I had somehow buried, things from when I was a kid, it brought up a lot of stuff,' Adrian said. 'I hadn't started out with that good foundation they are always talking about, and the horrible things ate me up so much I couldn't get close to God.'

This was reasoning Ella could understand, Adrian knew. It wasn't exactly how he saw it, but he sensed that if he wanted her to take in any of the story, he was going to have to tell it to her on her level, in a way that would suit the way she had been trained to listen to information by the church.

'What were the horrible things?'

Adrian paused before he answered. He didn't know that Ella wanted a solid answer. He didn't really know how much information to disclose. Every time there was a different response: when he told Harry, he was completely shocked and then supportive; with his grandparents there was some shock, but mostly support; his parents didn't seem to believe him when they had arranged the meeting with Fred and Timothy and essentially all that Timothy had said was to not tell too many people. So far, he had had a fifty/fifty response with helpful/not helpful responses. He ended up deciding to just tell Ella anyway. She could respond either way, and while it would hurt if it was like how his parents had responded, he had survived it before, and he could survive it again.

'When we went to the convention early last year, we were staying in with the workers. Do you remember that?'

Ella nodded. She had stayed in with two lovely sister workers. She didn't know who Adrian had stayed with, though.

'I was staying in a room with Fred.'

Ella suddenly got a shiver down her back and couldn't figure out why. She got the feeling whatever Adrian was about to say was going to change everything.

'Can I take your orders?' The waitress had appeared at their table. They both ordered a tea and a brownie. When they were alone again, Adrian continued.

'Everything was a bit weird from the moment I heard that I was going to be staying with him in that room. I was really reluctant to go into the room, but I had to put my stuff in the room, and at that point there weren't any other options. It got even stranger when I arrived in the room. We were sleeping on two separate beds, but the beds were weirdly close together. I knew they weren't originally like that because I had put the beds in there myself a few weeks before. When Fred came back from the bathroom, he just gave me this strange smile which sent shivers down my back, but I tried to ignore it as I put my stuff in a somewhat orderly fashion. Didn't want to seem too disorderly in front of a worker, you know?' His laugh was strange to Ella's ears.

'We went back out to have tea and he was being very friendly to me, making jokes, and I shook off my original feeling. I decided I was just tired and hypersensitive. It had been a long day. But when we went back to the room after tea, as I closed the door, I turned around and he was standing right behind me. That strange smile was back. He told me I had to be quiet, no matter what, as the overseer was in the room beside us and he was sleeping already. It wasn't a strange thing for him to say – it was actually true, but the way he said it, I wanted to just leave and go and sleep somewhere else. I went to leave, but his hand suddenly grabbed me and he twisted me into a lock. He must have done judo or something, but it hurt and I was helpless. "Remember, he's sleeping and he hates to be woken up," was hissed in my ear. It was really weird – it gave me flashbacks to when I was eight and he had done the same thing. I had pushed those so far down in my brain, but the flashbacks made me just freeze. I couldn't move, even if I tried. I couldn't scream; I was just stuck. Nothing worked, my body didn't want to cooperate.'

Adrian had told this story with a strange disconnection to this point. He was reciting something he had written down before he went to his parents about the whole thing, as Harry had suggested. This helped him to keep his cool that time, but there was something about the dismay on his sister's face that made him tune in to what he was saying. He broke down in tears. Real tears, rolling down his face, and he felt a shame and a guilt twist in his gut as he sobbed, feeling like a baby in the middle of his favourite café.

Ella felt sick. She wanted her brother to feel comfortable telling the story – knew that he needed to have a safe space to tell it – but she didn't know if she could cope with hearing the whole horrific tale. He hadn't finished, but she already knew how it ended. She had heard he had asked to change bedrooms the next day and that he wasn't able to. He had slept in that room for three nights in total.

'Adrian …' Her eyes matched her soft tone. 'You don't have to tell me if it's too upsetting. If you want to tell me another time, I'm here for you, but I don't want you to have to relive that any more than I'm sure you already do.'

He sobbed. It took him five minutes to get his breathing under control, by which time the waitress had brought their teas, brownies, and a handful of extra tissues. She looked concerned about him, but she didn't say anything. When Adrian felt more composed, he decided he wouldn't go into any more details. Maybe he would one day, if he ever got the guts to go to the police, but Ella was right. He didn't have to relive the details right now. She probably got the gist.

'It was horrible.'

'Three nights?'

He nodded.

Ella was silent for a moment, letting it sink in. It was difficult to comprehend.

'I'm so sorry you went through that. You know I love you and I'm here for you?'

He nodded, and she came over to his side of the table and gave him a big hug.

'I get why you left. Seeing him at convention, and then at every gospel meeting …' She shook her head. 'Do they know about this? The workers, or our parents?'

'Yeah, we had a whole meeting about it with him and Timothy … I haven't really talked about it since with Mum and Dad, but I got the feeling that they didn't really believe me, and Timothy told me I should keep it all under wraps. It was horrific having to be in that room, though, with Fred. At least I could talk this time though, use my voice just a little bit.'

'Keep it all under wraps? Should you not go to the police about it? You know, just in case he keeps doing it? Also, that is terrible. Why did you have to go into a room with that … that *man*.'

'Timothy said if I did that, I would be destroying the peace of the meeting, and I didn't want to do that.' Adrian looked a bit defeated by his words. He didn't believe them anymore. It was more that he hadn't wanted to have to relive everything by telling the police. He knew they would ask all these questions he just didn't want to have to think about. He had also never heard of any of the friends going to the police about another friend or a worker. It seemed like something you just didn't do. A few years ago, people had come out against the Catholic Church, claiming that various priests had abused them, so he knew it was possible. He had already got enough grief from his parents for just stopping going to meetings though. He would probably lose their support completely if he started talking about it.

'Timothy also said that we were a perfect church made up of imperfect people and that's why it happened.'

Ella felt a little bit reassured by this knowledge, but she had strong feelings about the fact that the police didn't know about this man. He was a danger to everyone he would stay with. Fred was a strong man, and if he had managed to overpower her strong, agile brother, he would definitely be able to overpower anyone else that he decided to. Also, the fact that her brother had also been attacked as a child was eating her up inside. She felt sick. She excused herself, went to the bathroom, and heaved a couple of times. When she came back, they sat in silence across from each other until Ella spoke.

'Adrian?'

'Yes?'

'I love you, you know that?' Ella's voice was soft.

'I do. Love you, too.'

'You do have to tell the Gardaí, though. I'll come with you if you want support, and if anyone asks, I'll stand behind you, but you have to tell them. It doesn't have to be today, but they should really know. Prevent it from happening to someone else.'

He stared at her. He hadn't expected this at all.

'Harry said that, too. I just can't tell the story in full yet. I also don't want this to affect anyone else.'

'The best way to ensure that is to report him.'

'I know, but it's hard.'

'It is. Of course, it is your right to not tell them. The thing is, and I know this is probably a horrible thing for me to say, but this is probably not just about you.'

'I will go. Can you give me time, though?' Adrian stared determinedly at the table as he spoke.

'Of course. Write it all down as well as you can remember before you go.'

'I will, thanks.'

There was a silence, then Ella spoke again. 'Adrian?'

'Yes?'

'It's not your fault.'

She saw him crumple and held her arms out. 'Can I give you a hug?'

He nodded and she walked around the table and hugged her taller, stronger, older brother, reduced to a shell by that man. She tried to support his weight as he laid his head on her shoulder and sobbed. She started crying, too.

'It's not your fault, I promise it's not. He's a hateful old man.'

He cried hard as she repeated those words, over and over. When he got too upset, she helped him to breathe, getting him to concentrate on each breath, bringing everything right back to the breath for both of them. In and out.

She had made up her mind by the time Adrian had started breathing normally. She reached into her bag and messaged Ryley and then her mum.

Going to be late. Will get tea before I come home x

She reached back into her bag and pulled out a notebook and a pen. The pen wouldn't write for the first couple of tries, and then it did.

'Okay. When we go to the police, we're hopefully getting the cogs in motion to prevent this from happening again. Tell me, in detail if you can, what happened and I'll write it down for you. I know you did this already, but in proper detail this time. Afterwards, we're going to go make you an appointment with the GP and try to get you a counsellor as soon as we can.'

She felt like an adult. She wrote down what he told her, word for word, writing as quickly as she could. Adrian had to stop sometimes to gather himself, and she waited patiently for him to be able to continue. When it seemed like it was becoming too much for him, she messaged Harry. She guessed he would want to be here to help her brother do this. She told Adrian Harry was coming and he nodded, took a deep breath, and continued. They had the whole statement written out when Harry arrived. She showed it to Harry, and he agreed that this was what Adrian had told him on that walk outside convention. They sat either side of Adrian, the third cup of tea and coffee going cold in front of them. No words had been exchanged for nearly ten minutes as the three of them just sat, staring into nothing.

Ella was processing it all, or at least attempting to. It felt like her whole life had been turned upside down. Never before had she been angry at a worker before. It felt odd, like her brain was trying to fight itself, even though she knew that, in this instance, the anger was perfectly justified.

Suddenly, Adrian took a breath and spoke.

'I want to go to the Gardaí. I want to go now.'

'Are you sure?' Ella looked up from reading through her notebook to check for coherency.

'Yeah. I feel ready. I also just want the first step to be over with.'

'I completely understand. We're right beside you.'

It had been really hard hearing the full story for Ella, about the level of twistedness that that man was. She felt awful that her brother had lived with this whole situation for a full year before telling anyone about it. She regretted all the times she had judged him and had thought of him as weak or giving in to temptation.

The police station was a scary building. When they entered, they all stood huddled in a run-down room which would have benefitted from a bit of paint, waiting behind a man who smelled like he had a drinking problem and who was holding a young girl by the ear. He was arguing with the policewoman, who was sitting behind a see-through barrier.

When it was Adrian's turn, Ella and Harry squeezed his hand and whispered support. The other pair then both filed in to give their own statements, trying to remember what Adrian had said and his actions since the incident. When it was all over, they made their way out, all standing on the steps outside the police station, none of them talking. They all moved slowly, thinking deeply about everything. Ella started walking towards a park that was nearby and Adrian and Harry followed her. None of them had any thought formed enough to create words to describe it. Ella found that she was thinking in fragments. She kind of wanted to just go home, but she guessed Adrian needed more support than that. They all jumped when her phone rang.

'Ella, where are you? It's a Saturday night – you can't be out too late.'

'Oh. Sorry, Mum, I lost track of time. Adrian isn't feeling very well. I'm going to stay with him until he feels better.'

'What's wrong with him?'

'He'll be okay. He's just a bit upset. He said he has told you guys about it.'

Silence. Then …

'You know he's possibly exaggerating about it all to make an excuse so he doesn't have to go to meetings anymore?'

Ella stared down at her phone. Adrian had said he suspected his parents felt that way, but she hadn't expected this level of denial from her parents.

'Mum, he isn't exaggerating, I don't think. I've never seen Adrian so upset, and I've seen the changes since it happened – I just didn't know what they were from.'

Silence

'Look, I know, Ella. I just … He is going to make a big fuss about this and … you just don't know the consequences …' She trailed off. 'Anyway, I suppose you can make your own decisions. When are you coming home?'

'I'll be home around nine.'

'Okay, just don't be too late. And I'm really not happy about you being out in the city on a Saturday night.'

Ella hung up and turned to Adrian.

'Well, the good news is that she doesn't completely disbelieve you …'

Adrian nodded.

'She still doesn't think it is a good idea to report it, though, does she?'

'No. She doesn't.'

'Ella, I think I should tell you something else before we go.' Adrian glanced at Harry, checking he was okay with it.

'What is it? I need to catch my bus in a couple of minutes.'

'I am bisexual. Don't tell Mum or Dad please, but Harry and I are in a relationship.'

Ella stared at her brother. She nodded and gathered her bag.

'Adrian, it has been a long day. I need to catch my bus. I love you, and I am so glad you went to the Gardaí today, but I really think you should both pray harder about that relationship.'

Ella gave her brother and his apparent boyfriend a quick hug, then walked quickly away. She got on the bus on autopilot and sat there, lost in her own thoughts the whole way home, to her family, where things made sense and her own boyfriend, who would be waiting to greet her with a big hug and a kiss.

Anna was still staring at her phone's blank screen five minutes after the call with her daughter had ended. She was feeling something uncomfortable but couldn't put her finger on what it was. She started as Justin ran in, looking for a pencil for a last-minute piece of homework.

'Just make sure you finish it before midnight.' She snapped as she picked the pencil up from under a blanket. Justin started and nodded. Anna was left standing alone.

Her heart felt heavy when she thought of her oldest son. She missed him during term time, but she felt like he was slipping from her, even when they were in the same area. He avoided her as much as possible and didn't make eye contact with her when they were talking. It was like he was afraid of her or something. She couldn't understand it. Anna knew that Adrian had lost out and prayed every morning and evening that he would see the error of his ways, but as time went on, she was finding it harder to shake the feeling that it was her fault that he had drawn back from her. And now her daughter was on Adrian's side. She hoped that Ella would have a good influence on her son. Shrugging her shoulders, she put the phone down on the table and went back to tidying the sitting room for the meeting tomorrow.

Chapter Sixteen

Ella still hadn't really processed everything that had happened five months ago on that day back in January. She had gone back to her parents' house and pretended that nothing had happened, sat in the missions and meetings, listening to the man who still disgusted her, and got on with life. Her leaving cert was that year, so she focused on that and her relationship with Ryley, which was better than ever. Things hadn't really progressed, as she still didn't feel comfortable doing any more than shirts off, but that was apparently enough for Ryley. He was still working for the O'Learys and loving it. As he was an Irish citizen, he was able to study there, much to Ella's delight. She kept in contact with Adrian and had visited him again a couple of times in between. She never told him about how much Fred was annoying her, though, as she didn't want to trigger anything in her brother. She never acknowledged the fact that he had told her of his relationship with Harry and never asked about it, and Adrian never brought it up again.

Adrian was doing slightly better. The counselling was helping him and his relationship with Harry was improved a lot by that. They were closer than ever before, and Harry had eventually helped Adrian clean out his room shortly after they went to the Gardaí with the information. It felt a lot better to be living in a clean space. As Harry's parents had kicked him out, they both arranged to rent a room in the house where Harry had been staying. They had also both lined up jobs for the summer. They wouldn't be living together next term. Both knew living together at college would be too intense for their relationship and they weren't yet ready for that, but they figured it was safe enough to share a house for a few months.

Fred had been detained by the police shortly after Adrian had made his statement, but he had apparently denied everything, as they had suspected that he would. It was a worrying time, but there were no immediate consequences to Adrian's reporting things that he could see, other than the gossip that Adrian heard about from time to time, criticising him for going to the police and sullying the good name of a respected worker. Timothy had ignored Ella when she came across him at Grace's house one weekend despite her going out of her way to glare at him, but otherwise it was relatively calm on that front for the moment.

Ella and Adrian spoke about it frequently, of course but there was no more news. Adrian told her that she could tell Ryley, whom she hadn't filled in yet, but she could never bring herself to do so. It was always sitting in the back of her head, ready for when she was about to fall asleep or to catch her off-guard, though. Even though half the friends in Ireland already knew on some level what had happened, few of them seemed to have the right end of the story. A surprising amount of them thought that they shouldn't have said anything to the police. A woman had even approached Ella one day after the mission and told her, 'Your brother would have been better off leaving it to the workers.' Ella just about resisted slapping the woman, but it had all angered Ella no end.

Meanwhile, Ella had started noticing things within the church that were irritating her more than usual. Where she had always felt that women should be able to say thanks for the bread and wine, it now bothered her that they couldn't. According to Ryley, they were allowed to in Canada, which made it even more confusing to her as to why they couldn't in Ireland. She secretly bought her first ever pair of jeans and wore them when on a date with Ryley one day. She had never been more scared of randomly coming across one of the friends, but at the end of the day, she felt triumphant about it. All the while, her parents pretended that nothing had happened to Adrian. Ella just let it pass, as she couldn't cope with it anymore.

Fred would say things in the meeting and she would actively argue against him in her head because she disliked him so much. He would say that the Truth was the only way to get to heaven and that other churches had to be wrong, and she would think, *well, how do you know that?* Unless he was including himself negatively in the message, she disagreed with his points wholeheartedly. In the very last mission, she sat relieved, having not noticed how much tension she had been holding all the time that that man was standing there in front of her. She had magically become sick on those evenings, developed headaches – sometimes real ones at the thought of seeing him – and had begged too much work. At one point, she had missed three weeks of missions in a row. This had led to a visit from Fred and his companion.

She was told that they were concerned that she was losing out and that she was going down the wrong path by prioritising her schoolwork too much. She had never told

the workers why she wasn't going to the meetings, so she
deduced her parents had arranged this meeting, as their
conversations weren't having the desired impact anymore.
She sat through the whole ordeal. When they were
finished, she found that, for the first time in her life, she
didn't want Jesus to help her to forgive this man. She
wanted to see him hurt for all of the damage he had caused
to her brother. She stopped trying to argue against his
every word, and had just stopped listening, concentrating
on homework exercises in her head, or counting the tiles on
the ceiling of the hall they were in – there were one
hundred and seventy to be precise, with ten lights – or
imagining not having to listen to him ever again. Strangely,
her mum had started treating Fred aloofly too, ignoring him
on purpose. It gave Ella a sliver of hope about it. It wasn't
enough, of course, but it was something.

Now, five months since she, Harry, and her brother
had gone to the police about Fred, it was convention time
again. Once again, she slept in the sleeping quarters beside
her friends. This time, she sat in the meetings beside Ryley
with her friends around them. But, for the first time in her
life, she couldn't help but feel slightly distant from the
whole process. When workers said certain things, she felt
like she was in a comic and there were question marks
popping out of the top of her head. Some things sounded so
ridiculous to her ears.

She was walking out of the first meeting when the
sister worker in charge of the convention grounds came up
to her.

'Ella, there you are. Could you fill in for Ivy with
the workers' tables? She's just been called to help with a

family emergency.' The sister worker looked up at her and smiled.

Ella felt a little bit trapped as her two friends watched her expectantly. Ryley was eating with those on the washup, so he was served earlier at a different table. That meant she wouldn't be eating with him anyway.

'Yeah, of course!' Ella said eventually. It was the only possible answer. She was generally well-behaved, wearing all the right clothes and hanging out with all the right people. Generally, she worked hard at the convention, so she understood why they wanted her to help out. She was a good option. She just didn't want to be anywhere near the man called Fred Angel. Walking over with the sister worker, she was given a quick run-down of what she should do, serving the workers. The workers tended to get slightly different food, with people often baking things specifically for them, but this was her first time participating in the process. She couldn't believe the preferential treatment Fred would be getting. Specific plates, cutlery – everything was well thought through just for the workers while the friends got whatever was going. She had known this was the case, but it just felt so unfair. The workers were meant to be equal to the friends, but it didn't feel that way.

Her job started with handing out the food and ensuring that the older workers had some assistance while serving the food. This seemed reasonable to Ella. Then she was to serve the tea and coffee. She went around the table, pouring the tea for the workers who wanted it. Fred wanted tea, so she poured it for him, 'accidentally' spilling it on the table. She apologised half-heartedly.

'Sorry about that, Fred,' Ella said flatly, wishing she could have poured the rest of the scalding water on him, wanting to cause him a little bit of the pain he had caused her brother and through him, her. But unfortunately, she wasn't a psychopath. She regrettably moved on and tried to ignore growing feelings of anger and frustration at the man. He was being so rude. He had barely acknowledged her presence, while other workers were being so polite and thankful for everything she did. She did her best to appear as though she weren't paying him any attention, but she noticed every word he said. Even as she tried to tune out his voice, it seemed to seep into every part of her body, creeping her out immensely. She looked at him once, unable to keep the feelings of hatred out of her gaze. She saw him look up, see her gaze and smirk. When she was finished serving the workers, she ate her own food quickly and went to the sleeping quarters and dug her head in the pillow. She felt like screaming. She had a strange feeling that she wanted to cause the maximum possible damage to that man.

Grace and Hannah walked into the sleeping quarters just as she was contemplating how she was going to cope with seeing him every day. She had seen something in that man's eyes, and she wanted to turn it into a fear, to make him feel some extent of how her brother had felt. She wouldn't do anything to hurt him physically of course, but a little bit of psychological torture would surely be acceptable, just to make him sweat. Grace came over and sat down beside Ella. She didn't seem to notice Ella's intense line of thought.

'Want to come on a walk? There's a group of us
going.'

Ella nodded. That would be a healthier way of
dealing with her emotions.

'Is Ryley coming?'

'Yep. I just saw him, and he was looking for you.'

She walked out and saw Ryley looking at her, with
a slightly concerned expression on his face. She walked
over to him, and they stood, holding hands as the rest of the
group gathered themselves and then set out. Ryley glanced
over at her, his eyebrows drawn together.

'Can I talk to you?'

'Of course, what's up?' Ella was immediately
worried. Was he going to break up with her? She knew she
hadn't been the most attentive girlfriend the last while.

'Is everything okay with you? You've been acting
distant since we arrived at the convention.'

She slowed down and looked at him. It was time to
be honest. They had been together long enough.

'No, actually, it isn't. But I can't talk about it here.
Can we go for a drive this evening?' Ella had finally got
her driver's licence that spring.

Ryley nodded. 'Of course, are you safe, though?
How worried should I be?'

'Honestly, don't worry too much about me, and our
relationship is fine, but I still need to tell you because I
don't think it is fair otherwise.'

'Okay, honey, I trust you.'

They kissed quickly and continued their walk,
catching up with Hannah and Grace and joining their
conversation.

That evening, they sat in the drive-through of the McDonalds down the road, ordering their food.

'It always feels weird to leave the convention grounds,' Ella commented. 'It's like we get into a bubble when we go to convention or something.' She said it every time she left, but she felt it as a relief this time where it had always felt like a shock previously.

Ryley nodded as she turned to pay at the next window. When they were sitting parked, eating their burgers and fries, Ella was gathering up the courage to tell him the whole story.

'I always like a break from the convention food, though. It has been one day of stew and bread and porridge and I'm already over it.'

Ryley murmured assent through a bite of his burger.

She paused, not wanting to speak the words aloud.

'So… I guess I should have told you this a while ago, but I never felt like it was my story to tell. Recently, though, it has felt like I am drifting away from the friends, like I have lost all of my love for the meetings.' She looked down at the steering wheel as she spoke. She was already feeling the tears coming on, but she tried to keep them down. She still had a long way to go.

Ryley looked at her, chewing thoughtfully.

'That sounds serious. I can't say I have been loving the meetings recently either but tell me your side first.'

Ella looked at him in surprise.

'Oh. Okay, well, I'd love to hear more about that at some point. But basically, it's because of something that happened to Adrian.' She told Ryley the whole story, leaving out the gory details, but outlining the way Adrian had been treated by the workers and how, since he had gone to the police, some of the friends had been spreading malicious rumours about him.

When she was finished, Ryley just looked at her. After a few moments, he spoke.

'That is not what I expected. Wow. That bastard.'

Ella blinked at the vocabulary he was choosing but didn't comment. She agreed with the word choice.

'I'm so sorry that that happened to your brother. Poor Adrian. I completely understand why you feel so disillusioned with it all … Huh. Is he okay?'

'Yeah, it has been a weird couple of months. He's doing okay. He's been to the GP and seen a therapist. He said that has helped.'

Ryley nodded.

'And how are you doing?'

'I've had a rough time of it, I'm not going to lie. I know it didn't happen to me, but I just feel so … so weak and helpless when I think about it. I wish I had known and stopped it.'

'Fred never hurt you, did he?'

'No … I did wonder 'cos Adrian had forgotten about so much until he was abused again, but I can't think of anything. Thankfully.' She took another couple of bites, then remembered. 'What was it you were saying about not loving the meetings either?'

'Oh right, yeah. I have been feeling a bit disconnected since I went back home. I never told you this, but basically my dad, who is really well respected by the people in the meetings, is an asshole.'

'An asshole?'

'An asshole. He is physically abusive to my mom, he yells at her, and used to lose his temper with us quite a lot. And now he has cheated on her as well. Several times. But she won't leave him. The workers have asked her time and time again to just stay with her husband, that God needs her to stay in her place, to forgive him over and over and over again. Basically, when I went home at Easter, I kicked dad out. The workers came over afterwards and told me not to do that, but I showed them my mum's bruises. Do you know what they said?' He was starting to raise his voice, and Ella watched him quietly.

'No, what did they say?'

'They said she had *never needed to go to hospital*. That meant that she was obviously safe enough … That she should stay with that man because she wasn't going to die at his hands. That she should forgive, seventy times seven, as Jesus had said.' Ryley seemed defeated when he finished talking.

'But shouldn't your dad have some responsibility here?'

'Yep. He got a slap on the wrist. Was asked if he was sorry, he said yes. They said okay, go back to your wife. This is why I think getting married just because you're too horny is a stupid fucking reason to get married.'

Ella nodded.

'I agree. I know I've been holding back with our sexual lives. I don't want to do something just because someone else wants it, but I'm ready to go further with you now.'

'Are you sure?'

'Yeah. It's not to say I want to have sex with you
tonight or something, but just soon. Not all at once, but we
can definitely take steps in that direction.'

He kissed her deeply.

'I love you, Ella.'

'I love you, too, Ry.'

It was the first time they had said it out loud. They
smiled at each other.

'I'm so relieved I was able to tell you those parts of
my life, and thanks for letting me see that part of you – it
can't have been easy.'

'It wasn't, but we have each other at least, don't
we.'

When they got back to the convention grounds, it
was well past lights out. They had gone for a walk in the
same park Harry and Adrian had gone to the last time.
They discussed everything, talking for the first time about
their fears and hopes in real detail. It was odd, Ella
reflected, how it had felt like it was a deep, meaningful
relationship before, but really it had been based on a very
superficial layer. They had both kept big details from each
other, in an attempt to fit in to what they had thought the
other had expected. But now their relationship was truly
deep and meaningful. They had bared their souls to each
other. Before they stepped out of the car, Ryley laid a hand
on Ella's shoulder.

'I don't know what the next while will bring –
whether we will stay in the meetings, or if we will leave.
But, either way, I really think that we should pray about it
and ask God for guidance. In a true way, not just a half

meaningful way that I have always prayed in, leaving half
the details out.'

Ella nodded, and they sat there, bowed, holding
hands and silently pleading that the God they loved would
love them enough to make it all make sense.

Somehow, they got through the next few days, spending
the evenings together. Ella felt slightly bad for her friends,
whom she felt like she was abandoning slightly, but Grace
had a boyfriend as well and Hannah was spending a lot of
time helping the workers with all the tasks. Thankfully,
Ella didn't have to serve the workers again, as the lady who
normally did it returned, the family crisis having been
averted. After the first meeting on the last day, the
workers' lists were handed out. When Ella glanced down at
the list in her hand, she saw Fred's name beside a different
country. He would be staying in the work for another year
at least, it seemed. They were still waiting on the police to
decide whether the case would be brought to court or not,
and it seemed like Fred and the overseers hadn't even
heard of it. They were actually moving him out of the
country. She stared at the lists for a few minutes, then ran
down to her car to call Adrian. She hardly noticed that
people were gathering around Hannah.

'Adrian …' she started as he picked up on the
second ring.

'What's wrong?'

'They're moving Fred to Nigeria.' Her voice shook.

'What? He's still in the work?' They had hoped that
the case would make them take him out of the work
entirely.

'Yeah, and it looks like they're trying to move him out before the case becomes public and he has to go to court.'

'How are they going to make him go to court if he's not even in the EU, never mind the country?'

'I have no idea. Adrian, you have to call your case manager. See if they can get the date for the decision moved forwards, because once he leaves the country, they may never see him again. We have to stop him before he does any more damage.'

'I'll do that and message you when it's done. Can you send me a photo of the workers' list?'

She sent it quickly.

'Thanks, I got that now. Wait, is Hannah going in the work?'

'What?' Ella looked at the list again. She had only been looking for one name when she had read the list, but there it was. Her best friend's name. On the list. Ella's heart sank and she didn't understand why. She should be delighted. She took a slightly shaky breath and geared herself up to go and congratulate her best friend. It felt like a loss.

She walked slowly over to join the circle of people. Most of them were leaving, having said their congratulations and moving on to the next worker. Ella overheard the occasional comment, people saying how nice it was, and someone who was in the first field she was going to, getting excited about it. As she made eye contact with her best friend, her heart sank even more. It was strangely difficult seeing Hannah so happy about something that, just six months before, Ella herself would

have been delighted about for her. It wasn't that Ella
wanted to bring anyone else down the path she felt she was
going, but she didn't want her friend stuck either. All the
same, she plastered on a smile for her friend. She loved her
more than enough to do that, to support her.

'Hannah! I just heard the news!'

'I know, it's such a brilliant feeling that I can
finally tell you. I wanted to tell you so many times this
year, and every time I just about managed to keep it in!'
They hugged. Hannah was radiating with a sort of joy Ella
had never seen in her before. She was happy her friend was
so delighted with her decision.

Hannah quickly told her the whole story. She had
felt moved to go into the work for two years already, but
she had wanted to finish school first. While she didn't have
any degree or anything that she could fall back on, she
trusted that the Lord would provide and that this would be
the right choice for her. When Hannah came back from
Nigeria, she had spent a lot of time with some of the
workers who were staying with her parents at that point.
That time had made her think a lot about the work. Those
sister workers had referred consistently to the need of the
harvest and it had felt like that truly was a sign from God.
She hadn't told anyone apart from Timothy until she had
had to quit school, and then she had only told her parents
so they would stop threatening to enrol her straight back in
college. Even though she had had that negative experience
in Nigeria, Hannah told Ella, she wanted to change things
like that and felt that she could.

'It's worth it in the end, Ella – it is so worth it, you
have no idea.'

She knew it would be hard, Hannah continued. She had sold most of her belongings already and had given the money to the workers. She wasn't going to see her family often, especially as she had been sent five hours away from them, and she might even have to go away for years on end if Timothy decided to send her somewhere else. Mostly, though, she would miss seeing her two best friends, and indeed all of her friends as often. She knew that their dynamics would change once she went in the work and they would suddenly look at her differently.

'No!' Ella interjected. 'I'll always see you as my best friend, Hannah.' They hugged.

Hannah had been so nervous that convention, she admitted, waiting for someone to accidentally share the news too early, or for her to give it away herself. Most of all, though, she felt a peace that this was the right decision for herself and she immediately acted happier and more relaxed the moment the news came out, as she had seen others before her do.

They chatted about where Hannah was going to go and who her companion was – Ella didn't remember who the sister worker was any more than Hannah did, as she had only been seven the last time she had been at the convention.

'I'm so sorry that Adrian has lost out. Was it the world that got him?'

It had come from nowhere, one moment they were normal, and then suddenly she was talking about Ella's brother and judging him for having been too weak to fight against the world.

'You heard the rumours, I'm sure,' Ella said. 'Fred sexually abused him.'

'Oh, but that's not true, is it? I assumed they had made that whole story up.'

Ella just looked at her.

'The only lie here is that they are saying he's lying about it.'

'I didn't mean to offend you, I'm sorry. I had no idea.' Hannah looked genuinely sorry.

Ella sighed.

'I know you didn't, but Fred shouldn't be in the work. He could be attacking all sorts of children and now they're sending him to Nigeria to get him out of the way.'

'Oh, I'm so sorry. He was right to report him then. I would say something to stop that, but I really can't. I … I just can't.'

Ella knew this was true. Only the senior male workers made any sorts of decisions. If Hannah said something now, she could cause problems down the line, and she had probably just given all of her possessions and money to the brother workers. But anyway, they couldn't do anything about it right now. There was one more meeting left in the convention and they both went over to their usual seats. Grace was busy childminding, as her sister had a two-year-old and a five-month-old and they were quite the handful, but Grace had come over to give Hannah a hug and a promise to talk more about it after the meeting when the kids had gone. She saw Ryley for the first time, and he gave her a questioning look.

'All good? I didn't see you at all,' he asked, looking at her closely.

'I'll tell you later,' she whispered and turned towards the platform.

They sat down, a familiar feeling settling over Ella until she looked at the list. Fred was speaking second in the meeting. She tried to breathe through the stress of having to listen to him again. Ryley glanced over at her, seemingly aware of her reaction to the man. He reached over and squeezed Ella's hand. Hannah, on the other side, tapped her knee in support.

Ella could barely listen to the words that were being spoken. She was furious at the fact that this man was still winning, that her brother didn't even have a choice to be here because of this man's wrongdoings. When it was time for Fred to speak, she mirrored her brother's actions from two years ago and put her head down as close to her knees as possible, trying to distract herself until she unwillingly started listening to what the man was saying.

'I know you all already know that the internet is a bad place full of worldly things, but I recently heard that people were writing books about us. These books should not be read. God has written only one book for us, and that book is the Bible. Any other book is not something that God wants us to waste our time on. You know, Lot was a time waster …'

Ella stopped listening. She had decided she wanted to buy that book. Anything to piss off that man, Ella thought, feeling slightly guilty about the language she was allowing to enter her heart. The rest of the meeting didn't stand out much to her, but as she considered what he had said, the words of that worker, Graham, speaking against what others had written on the internet came to her. At the time she wanted to avoid it with all her might, but now she wondered what was on there that was getting Fred so worried.

That evening, when they got home, Ella got out her phone. She went onto Google and realised she didn't know what to search for.

'*The workers*' she typed in. A dictionary reference, an app. Not what she was looking for.

'*The Truth*' – nothing related to the Truth.

'*The way, the Truth*' – a lot of Bible verses.

'*Two-by-two workers*' – a Wikipedia page called 'Two by twos'. That might be something? She clicked on it and found a picture of three men who looked like they could be workers. She started reading. She read how it originated in the nineteenth century and nearly stopped reading. The truth had been around since Jesus's time, so this couldn't be it. But then something caught her eye. It said that among its members, it was often called 'the Truth' or 'the way'. That seemed oddly familiar to what they called it among themselves. Ah, but it was started by some guy called William … No, it wouldn't be it. But then it mentioned workers. Ella stuck with the article, reading how a man called William Irvine split off from the Faith mission and preached the gospel according to how Jesus had told His disciples to go in Matthew 10.

William went out and recruited members, getting most of those who joined to give everything up and go and follow Jesus, similar to the Faith mission structure, except they didn't need to give all their belongings away within the faith mission. He had gained a lot of interest very quickly, it seemed – Ella had heard stories from older people telling how they used to have missions filled with people. He had called other churches wrong quite openly, apparently using strong language, causing enough attention for a member of the British government to offer to join the church, just to get the members to stop insulting the other churches so much. She read about how the newspapers had written about their baptisms, how they had sent people abroad, and then how in 1904, just seven years after its start in 1897, people weren't told to sell all anymore; they could have homes for the workers and those who went in the ministry were the only ones who would have to leave all. That also explained how there used to be so many workers, Ella thought.

In 1914, just seventeen years after William had started the religion, he was kicked out for starting to preach about the end of the world. He apparently predicted that Jesus was coming back in 1914. His friend, Edward Cooney, who had been there from the start, wasn't listening to the new order of the organisation that William had set up, and this meant that he was also kicked out, as he wanted to go where he wanted to and preach to whomever he wished. Ella recognised this story, as Grace had told her that's why people sometimes called them Cooneyites – Cooneyites were the product of Cooney's being removed and starting his own church. She read how people were kicked out of the church for trying to argue with the workers about being from the beginning and that the church had tried to disappear out of the public view.

The biggest theme since the early 1900s was that they had hidden as much as they could from the public. For an organisation that claimed it wanted to gain more members, it had left a very poor trail for those wanting to see if it was trustworthy to follow.

She found other websites; read other stories about incredible things the friends had done – a story of someone who had to wear black tights their whole life stood out to her as Ella had never known this was a rule. She read stories by people that Fred had said were full of anger at the church, but all she could see was pain. Most of the people writing these blogs had been hurt by the two-by-twos, as she now thought of them. The name itself put a different spin on the view she had of her beliefs. She now wondered where those small envelopes of money that were passed at convention and gospel meetings were actually going. There was so little transparency about how it all worked. She sent some links over to Ryley.

Look at this!!

She called Adrian again.

'What's up, Ella?'

It was Harry who'd answered.

'Hey, Harry, is Adrian there?'

Ella and Harry hadn't spoken since the day they had reported everything. She still didn't know how she felt about them being a couple, but her thoughts that had stopped working were now running at five times the speed. She decided it wasn't that important right now.

'Yeah, I think he's in the kitchen.'

'Who is it?' She heard Adrian's voice getting louder and steps getting closer.

'Ella.'

'Oh! Hey. Ella. Everything okay?'

'Yeah, well sort of, I think. I told Hannah and Grace about what happened – everyone apart from them and Ry think that the falsified version is the right version unfortunately.' Ella had told Grace after the meeting, as they helped with clear up. Now she was sitting in her room, far away from where her parents and Justin were sitting in their living room. Their stairs were so creaky, she'd be able to hear them if they came within earshot.

'Ah, what did they say?'

'All three want to give you a hug. They believe you, of course.'

'I'm glad.'

'Adrian, have you ever googled anything about the Truth?'

'No actually, why?'

'Google it. There's a Wikipedia article.'

'Oh, okay. I'll look it up later.'

'Adrian, I know I asked why you left before, but how did you leave it? How did you stop going to the meetings?'

Adrian paused for a moment before replying.

'I just couldn't cope anymore … It was too much. Umm, I don't know, it was really hard … I still haven't figured it all out.'

'I get it, it's weird, we have always been told that it is easier to leave, while staying takes work, but I feel like I have been floating for the last while. Just going half-heartedly. It felt a lot easier to do that, you know; I still have all my friends and our parents, but recently, I don't know … I … yeah, I can't imagine still going to the meetings? But also, I can't imagine leaving? There are so

many of the friends whom I love, who are genuinely nice
people who do so much for others. I don't want to lose
them, you know? I don't know what to do. I want to just
skip this part and know what I am going to decide.
Anyways, you don't need to worry about that; we need to
focus on keeping Fred in the country before they can whisk
him off somewhere else.'

Adrian was silent for a minute.

'Ella, that's a lot.'

'Yeah …' Her voice trembled and she took a
couple of deep breaths.

'I hope you can figure it out without the pain that I
had, but I know that isn't very likely.'

'Dude, I'm not bisexual, nor have I been assaulted.
You had it worse.'

'It's not really a competition.' Adrian's voice was
gentle.

'For what it's worth, I'm sorry, though.'

'What for?'

'I should have supported you more … I don't know.
I feel like I just stepped aside and let Mum and Dad just
kick you out. Maybe I should have done a sitting protest or
something, not eaten for a year. I should have stood in their
way, made them support you.'

'Ella …'

'Yeah?'

'Thanks. But you helped me a lot. You did all you
could with the information you had.' Adrian's voice stayed
soft as he comforted his little sister over the kilometres.

Ella was now actively struggling with not outright
crying.

'And Adrian?'

'Hmm?'

'How are things with you and Harry?'

'Good, thanks.' Adrian sounded surprised.

'He treats you well?'

'He does. He really does.'

'Good. I'm glad.'

When they hung up, Ella sat on the edge of her bed. She felt like she needed to be doing something, and now. She went back onto her phone and found a group for those who had left. She saw stories from different people. She also saw the book mentioned by the worker. *The Church Without a Name* seemed like an apt title. She ordered it to her friend's parents' house after she sent her a quick message. Then she called Ryley, who had gone back to the O'Learys for the week before the gathering up north.

'How are you doing, Ella?'

'I don't know. I really don't know. I don't know anything anymore, that is honestly how it feels.'

'I can imagine. I feel the same to be honest. How are they going to keep Fred in the country?'

'I don't know. I just don't know. This country's laws are made more complicated than they need to be and no google search is answering our question.'

'Hmm. That is frustrating. Hey, are you free tomorrow afternoon? I'm not needed for milking, so I can get an afternoon off. Do you want to hang out?'

'Yeah, that sounds good, and my parents will be working, and Justin is at his friend's house, so we'll be home alone.'

'Oh, I like the sound of that, talk to you tomorrow.'

'Yep! Love you!'

'Love you, too.' They hung up and Ella went downstairs, grabbed a snack, and a book to read and went back upstairs. She stood in the doorway, when the reality of the workers' ignoring her brother's experience suddenly hit her. She threw the book that she had been holding across the room, where it hit the wall and landed on the bed. She was suddenly filled with so much rage at the whole situation, she didn't know what to do with herself. She wanted to scream, but she knew that that would attract too much attention, so she slipped downstairs, put on a pair of shoes, and ran out of the door as fast as she could.

She sprinted out of the front gate and into the neighbours' field. She ran down the hill all the way to the small stream at the bottom, where she knew she was out of earshot of everyone in the area, and she screamed and shouted and dropped down on the grass and pummelled it. She wished she could punch Timothy and Fred and all of the people who were on Fred's side. She could have killed in that moment as she tried to get rid of the intense feeling that she was experiencing. She didn't even know what word worked in this instance. She just felt. Her body was shaking. It felt like it was coming in waves, hitting her again and again how unfair it all was. How backwards.

It was just pure injustice, and Ella wanted to change it, to make it better for those younger ones, so that no one else would be hurt, but she felt so stuck. Eventually, the pain and anger subsided, and she just felt scared and hurt. She sat on the grass, so drained from everything. She had read about other cases on a website linked to the friends, called Wings for Truth. It had story after story of people who had been put in the same situation as Adrian, by workers or friends. She had read of other instances, where the parents of kids just wanted to sort it out among themselves, not involve the authorities because apparently the workers were trained and competent at that.

Very fucking competent, she thought, *they didn't even want to remove Fred from the work, just move him somewhere else, move the problem.* If she moved in with Ryley, or if they had a kid before they got married, the workers would treat that as the most extreme sin. Even for those who were transgender, bisexual or gay – people like Adrian – were treated like they were committing one of the seven deadly sins, while those who were actually harming others were moved to a more convenient spot instead of following the logical route of getting the law involved.

Ella was frustrating herself thinking about all of the injustices. She thought again of Ryley's poor mum, asked to stay in the house with her abuser, just for the appearances of the whole organisation. She knew that the same was probably happening in Ireland, too, although no one talked about it. Domestic abuse was probably so much more common than they knew.

She remembered being beaten as a child – how, if they were too cheeky, or too loud in the meeting, they would be removed and slapped. She couldn't understand that. Kids are so innocent; they often just do what their instincts tell them. They explore the world themselves, are active – why would they slap a child just for being themselves? Ella thought of a kid she had seen at the convention who had just been playing in the mud with their friends, and who was given a good walloping in relatively plain site.

And the workers, with no kids of their own, and no training, they advise it, she shook her head. So many problems. She didn't even know what to focus on anymore. It was all so messed up. The weird thing was that until that Christmas, she hadn't even questioned any of these things. She buried her head in her hands again.

After she had paced several times, trying to make sense of her own thoughts, she was thoroughly shattered and made her way back home, to her house on the hill. When she got to the door, it was locked.

'Shit,' she mumbled under her breath. 'Shit shit shit shit.' She didn't even have her phone on her.

She went around and tried the other door; it was locked, too. No open windows, nothing she could climb through. After sitting on the back step, she decided to try yelling. She felt exhaustion take over and briefly considered sleeping outside.

'Hello!' she shouted, as loud as she could, and banged on the door. 'Anyone awake?'

She saw a light turn on in her parents' bedroom. She kept shouting until she saw the lights turn on in the hall, and the stairway.

Her mum opened the door groggily, in her pyjamas.

'Ella, what on earth are you doing out here at this time?'

'Sorry, Mum, I went for a walk.' She slipped past her mum and headed up the stairs.

'A walk?' she heard her mum repeat as she was relocking the door. 'Why in the name of goodness would anyone go for a walk at one am?'

Crap, Ella thought. She had been out of the house for over three hours somehow. She slipped into her pyjamas and climbed into bed. She was in for a rough night.

Chapter Seventeen

Ella ran out to greet her handsome boyfriend, who was striding across their front lawn. It was a beautiful day and she was delighted to see him, to spend some time with him and distract herself from the confusion that she felt deep within. They embraced and Ella led him inside.

'It's gorgeous weather,' she said, 'but first we need to take advantage of our time alone.'

They hadn't really had a lot of chances to be home alone recently. It had been busy, but her mum had picked up more hours at work since Justin had got older and was going to be away from home more often. Ryley had been busy, too, helping with silage, the ploughing, and spreading slurry and fertiliser, but he was off today, as they had just finished their last cut the week before. Ella had also got a job since January, in an attempt to save some money before college, so their weekends had been shortened, but she was swapping her hours to during the week, which she was thankful for now she was finished with school.

They locked the front door and shut the doors from the hall to the front door to make sure they wouldn't be surprised. Ella took Ryley's hand and led him up the stairs. She had bought some nice underwear a while ago and hid it under her mattress for this very occasion. She had just showered and could see that Ryley had done the same. They sat beside each other on the bed, kissing. Ryley slowly lowered her flat onto the bed, so they were making out properly. They paused as Ryley lifted Ella's T-shirt over her head, exposing her skin to the air, creating goosebumps across her chest and stomach. He reached behind her and unhooked the bra as their kisses deepened.

'Nice bra,' he murmured against her lips.

'Thanks, I got it especially for you,' she whispered back.

He made a satisfied sound and took it off. His lips left hers as they went to explore her bare chest. His lips explored her collarbone as his hands took in the breast. Then his lips followed his hands, dropping down slowly to her breast. He nibbled and licked, down to the nipple, which he teased with his tongue. Her hands reached down to the bottom of his shirt and brought it up over his head. He sat up slightly and helped her, then went back to exploring. His eyes widened as she took his hand down to the hem of her skirt. His gaze met hers, checking to see that she wanted this. She nodded.

'Please …'

He lifted her skirt, and slowly moved his hand up her thigh, higher and higher until it met the bridge. He slipped his fingers under the underwear.

'Tell me what you like.' His voice was hoarse.

'Move your fingers up, left a little bit. Yeah, there. Now gently rub it. Yes, like that.' She tried to relax into it. Slowly she began to feel the familiar building sensation. His mouth was still exploring her nipple.

'Can I go down on you? Or try it?'

'Yeah, go for it!' She helped him remove her skirt.

He sat back slightly and took her in. 'You're stunning, Ella.'

'You're not so bad yourself,' she said and winked.

He lowered himself between her legs and kissed her thighs, working his way up to the edge of her underwear. He took it off and kissed the area, before licking.

'Down a bit,' Ella instructed. 'A little bit more. Now to the left. Yep, there.' She moaned softly as he hit the right spot. He used his tongue to bring her up to the point, stopping a couple of times on the way to tease her with kisses on the inner thighs, but eventually she reached the climax and enjoyed the intense release that came with it.

He came up beside her.

'That was so good … You're really good at that!'

'Thanks! Not bad for a first time, eh?' He grinned.

She undid his belt buckle and lowered his trousers, taking in the shape under his boxers. She ran her hand over it gently, before lowering his boxers. She had never seen a penis before and wasn't sure which compliment worked.

'You have a really nice …' she said with a gesture. 'You're very handsome in general.'

His penis was bigger than she had really imagined and she was struggling with the idea that it would fit in the space that she couldn't even fit a small tampon in yet.

'I don't know how you're going to fit, though,' she said. 'You're quite big.'

'Thanks,' he laughed. 'We don't have to go the whole way just yet if you want.'

'No, I want to, I just don't really know … how to handle it … Or anything about it really? Could you teach me?'

He laughed gently. 'Yeah, of course I will.' His eyes met hers, and she could see the kindness behind them.

'How did you learn about how to … you know?' Ella watched as his gaze dropped. He shifted a little before answering.

'Well, I watched porn and also you directed me quite well.'

She nodded. The book hadn't been helpful as far as this bit was concerned.

'I have a condom if we want to go further, but we don't have to,' he said as he showed her how to grasp it. 'The head is the most sensitive, so when you're doing it with your hand or your mouth, focus on the head.'

She nodded and followed his guidance.

After testing it in her hand a couple of times, she brought her mouth down to join it. It was big but manageable. She brought him to his own finish line.

Afterwards, they got dressed in case someone came in by accident and lay beside each other, cuddling. It had been a welcome distraction and Ella felt happy about her decision. She wasn't yet ready to go any further, but they could have fun like this.

That evening, she knelt at the side of the bed as she had so many times. This time, though, her mind was blank. She just couldn't think of what to say. God had hurt her so many times, she felt. She didn't know what to say to him. She just knelt there. She had knelt at the side of her bed so many times, mostly just repeating something over and over again. Every so often she got inspiration for a particular cause, but right now she didn't have anything to say to a God. She got back into her bed. Then back out of bed and knelt again, suddenly afraid of her thoughts in case Jesus would come back that night. She stayed there for a minute, trying to think of anything she might want to say to a God who had sent that man to abuse her brother. She got back in bed. She decided she was okay to face Jesus without talking to him tonight. She had said enough – grovelled at God's feet enough to skip it just this one time. She didn't feel bad about what she and Ryley had done that day. She didn't experience the waves of guilt she had expected. Instead, she had made a decision for herself and it had been empowering. She should do it more often.

Chapter Eighteen

They were up the mountains, watching a sunrise together, when it finally hit Ella.

'I have to leave the meetings, I can't continue anymore,' she said, turning to Ryley, who had been standing silently at her side, just taking in the beauty.

He nodded and put his arm around her.

'I might lose all my friends.'

'I'm sure you won't.'

'But I might …' She sat down on the rock they had been standing on. She hadn't ever truly accepted it before.

It was the end of September, and they had both started their courses at Queens, the University in Belfast. Ella was studying music as she had always dreamed, and Ryley was studying Biochemistry. They had their accommodation sorted out, living in the same apartment complex. Fred had been able to leave the country that week, too, much to everyone's annoyance and frustration. He had signed an agreement to appear in court the next March, however, which was something. They were taking what they could get at this point.

But in the here and now, Ella was heartbroken. The decision was a painful one. She was able to take in the beauty, but it was only making her feel the pain deeper. Ryley sat behind her and wrapped his arms around her. They had had sex for the first time the week before, and although it had been slightly painful, Ella felt no change to how she was as a person, unlike what she had originally expected from the experience. She had even enjoyed it the second time and each time since.

Ryley rested his chin on her head and she relaxed back into his embrace, feeling so muddled with all the emotions.

'That's it, let it out,' he said softly as her tears fell. 'Let all the pain out.'

When the sun disappeared, they stood and wiped the dirt off their trousers. Ella looked up at Ryley.

'What do you think you will do?'

'I'm leaving, too. I decided at the convention. I kept going to the meetings 'cause I was at the O'Learys,' but I couldn't keep it up. I like the friends here okay, but I dunno, the workers haven't exactly acted very well, and some of the friends have been kind of bitchy.'

Ella nodded. She had suspected that.

They walked back down the mountain hand in hand. On the way down, they discussed all the ways it was all 'kind of fucked up,' as Ryley put it. They were both swearing a lot more recently.

'I mean, you go there and you get told that you're this horrible person, and that's their whole thing. Make you believe that you can't do shit on your own. That you need their particular God and that there is no other way. You know, I was thinking about how abusive that shit is the other day. They make you rely on them because of them telling you that you need God and you need the workers to get to God.'

'I don't even know what to think about God anymore,' Ella said thoughtfully. 'He is like this big man who is apparently all good, but do you see all the stuff that happens? Maybe it is because of the way we were brought up to think about Him, but I'm not a huge fan of Him right now.'

'I get that – it's all so mixed in with each other, it's hard to separate the factors out.'

'Yeah, exactly.'

'How am I going to tell my parents about this? It's going to break their hearts.'

'I don't know, you're going to have to figure that out unfortunately.'

'I am, aren't I. Have you told your mum?' Ryley had stopped all contact with his dad.

'Yeah, I called her. She didn't take it well, but she will be okay. Hey, at least you don't live at home anymore.'

'I know, but I had kind of hoped I would be able to go home every so often. Like Adrian only came home three times this whole year. Mum and I went over to visit him a couple of times, as you know, then Mum stopped when she found out about Harry and their relationship. But I don't want to end up like him. I know my parents have made mistakes, but I still want to have that contact with them, even if it isn't really Adrian's fault that that happened.'

He nodded.

'I completely understand, honey.'

It took a lot of time and conversations for Ella to accept her choice, it turned out, but once she was fully decided, it was just before Halloween. She sent a message to the elder of the meeting that she had been going to. And she and Ryley both stopped going. They both agreed that they still loved many people in the church, but at the end of the day, it wasn't worth all of the problems that were supported instead of condemned by the church.

A month after they eft, Ella went to get her ears pierced and bought her first necklace. Both were big steps, but she enjoyed the freedom. She had mixed emotions as she looked at herself in the mirror, finding it hard to recognise herself in the mirror. She was trying to figure out who she was as a person in general though, so it was to be expected. Overall though, she felt a happiness that was louder and lasted longer than the constant quiet voice of her upbringing. She had half expected for the feeling of satisfaction to last only a short while, as that was what they were told. It wasn't true, though – she was happier overall, other than when she was reminded of what had happened to her brother, and she felt less guilt for enjoying the small things in life.

Chapter Nineteen

When they got the call that their grandmother Poppy was sick, Ella and Adrian both rushed to her side. She had had a sudden heart attack. There had been some issues between the parents and their children, especially when Adrian had finally told his parents about his relationship with Harry. This was more important, though. When Adrian had called Ella on the way to the hospital, explaining his worries, she had told him to just come anyway.

'You may regret it if you don't, Adrian. We don't know how long she may have left. I know it will be tough, but dealing with the trauma of not seeing her at this point may be a lot harder to process.'

He had agreed, so they met in Dublin and went down to Cork together. Harry and Ryley were also on their way, but as they were both in Belfast that weekend – both for separate reasons – it would take them a lot longer to get there. Ella had been in Dublin at a concert for her school, so it was just a short drive to meet with Adrian.

When they arrived at the hospital, they found their grandmother in the ICU and attached to a lot of scary-looking machines. Peter was in the room beside his mother, and his father was on the other side. They were only allowing two people in the room at a time, Anna explained when they met her outside.

When it was time to go in, both of them went in together. Justin had been in before they had arrived to say his goodbyes.

'How is she?' Ella asked him.

'Not good. She doesn't think it'll be long either.'

Adrian and Ella walked in, holding hands – something they hadn't done since they were children, but they both needed support.

'Hi, Granny,' Ella said as she sat on a chair at her grandmother's bedside. Adrian sat, too. 'I heard you've been giving us all quite the fright.'

'Yes, well I have to keep you all on your toes, you see.'

They chuckled, but there was no humour in it.

'I know you are both quite worried about me dying, but don't worry, I'm quite ready for it. I have been my whole life.'

They nodded. They weren't about to argue with a person who might be dying.

'I am quite worried about you two, about how you have left the most important thing, but I still love you both, you know that.'

They nodded, tears coming to Ella's eyes.

'I don't think you should stay in that relationship, though, Adrian. I feel that God is quite upset with you.'

Well, that's ruined the moment, Ella thought.

'Mm hmm,' Adrian replied, noncommittally.

'I am more than ready to go home though. I think that it will not be long. I have lived a long life and seen a lot, and I'm ready to face my reward, if God is willing.'

They chatted a little longer until there was a knock at the door.

'The workers are here.'

'Oh, how nice of them. Well, it has been lovely speaking to you both, but I quite want to see the workers. I love you both, you know that.'

They told her they loved her too, hugged her, and left. They passed the workers in the hall – Timothy and an older man. Ella and Adrian didn't acknowledge the workers' presence, just walked straight past them, ignoring their greeting. Ella told Anna that they were going to get a coffee – it had been such a long journey and it could turn into a long night. Anna nodded, and Ella and Adrian set off down the corridor, following the signs to the cafeteria.

When they were far enough away, Ella exploded.

'I cannot believe that. She just kicked us out? For the workers? They are more important to her than we are! I should have known that, but that they would even ask to be let in when we were visiting our *dying* grandmother.'

'I know, it's fucking ridiculous.' His head was bowed as they stood in line.

'It was stupid what she said, Adrian. Don't pay her any heed – she's just an old woman from a different generation who has been in a cult all her life.'

He nodded.

'It just makes it so much harder, you know? Like we have spent a lot of time with our grandparents on that side, and they are always kind of judgemental. They are nice enough people, but ever since I left, I always have a funny taste in my mouth after I see them.'

'I have it, too,' said Ella.

Her phone rang, and she picked up. It was Ryley

'Where can we find you guys?'

'We're in the cafeteria at the moment. We're just getting something to eat and some coffee if you want some energy before you go up there.'

'Is everything okay?'

'It has been better, but we'll be okay. Just come on up when you can.'

They were ordering their coffee and sandwiches when Ryley and Harry walked into the cafeteria. They joined Ella and Adrian in the queue, receiving a couple of dirty looks from others behind them in the line.

'How are you both doing?'

'We've been better, not gonna lie.' Adrian replied as Ryley and Harry ordered their food.

'What's wrong?' asked Harry.

'Well, Granny started on her homophobia, and then after we'd just been in a minute or two, the workers arrived and she kicked us out so she could spend time with her heroes,' said Ella.

'Yeah, one of whom is definitely an enabler for a child sex abuser, so you know, we are having a brilliant day.' Adrian thanked the lady at the canteen, who had handed them their food, and they moved down the line to pay.

'That's … shit.'

'Yep, you're telling us.'

Harry shook his head. 'It just never stops, does it? It always has to make everything more complicated. Like when my granny died, it was before I came out as gay and left the meetings and I was still pushed to the side for the workers. They are apparently more important than the family themselves.'

'Yeah, well, I guess they are meant to be the saviours, you know? They are meant to be the way to get to God, the way they've all set it up—'

'Hey, we'll get that. You're going through, enough,' Ryley interrupted Adrian as he was about to pay, pushing him gently to one side.

'Oh no, don't worry about it at all.'

'I insist. You go and sit down; I'll be over in a minute or two.'

Adrian and Ella went to sit down. Ella glanced down at her phone. Six missed calls from her mum. Shit. She had forgotten to take her phone off silent. She called Anna back, dreading the response. No reply.

'Lads, I think we need to get back.' She showed them the phone. They nodded, grabbing their food.

Ryley was just walking over. 'What's—'

Ella showed him the phone and he nodded, taking his food from her. At least they had all got their food to go. They rushed through the hospital, walking briskly through the corridors, until Ella realised they were lost.

'I don't recognise this door, I think we need to go back a bit.'

They turned around, found the right corridor, and walked quickly down it. Anna and Justin were standing outside the ICU, consoling their dad. Ella's heart sank. They looked up as they approached.

'Is she …?'

'She's gone.'

'But … we were just talking to her – she was sick but she didn't seem like she was dying? How? Are you sure?'

They nodded.

'Yeah, she had another big heart attack when the workers were in with her, not long ago.'

They all just stood there, not sure what to do. Anna reached her hand out to her two oldest, who both joined the group limply. They just couldn't comprehend it. They had just gone for a coffee and some food. Their sandwiches felt like a waste.

The next while passed in a blur for them all as they went home and made plans for the funeral. They thankfully didn't see the workers again, as both Adrian and Ella were so angry that they had taken those last precious moments away from the family. Even though it was complicated, even though they had both felt anger towards their grandmother in the last few moments of her life, they had still loved her. They were both glad that those had been their last words to her. Ryley and Harry were supportive, and both felt a loss, as they had both known her well – Harry had spent a lot of time at her house when they were younger and Ryley had spent many Sundays at their place.

Their grandfather was making most of the decisions for the funeral, but they could all see that it was having a big effect on him. He had been standing outside, and had seen the last moments of his wife's life through a window. The suddenness of it all was hurting him. Before any of them could truly process what had happened, the funeral was arranged, the notice sent out in the papers. People started showing up, close friends of their parents and uncles, and they helped clear out Ella, Adrian, and Justin's house, tidying everything and putting things where they couldn't find them. People brought food over, and Ella and Anna tried to figure out where to put all of the food, which was mostly sandwiches, in preparation for the wake.

They went to bed early that night. Ryley and Ella were allowed to stay at home, in separate rooms of course, but Harry and Adrian weren't allowed to sleep at their parents' home and had to stay at the house of a childhood friend of Adrian's, whom he had kept in contact with. Ella didn't sleep much that night. She kept tossing and turning, thinking of her grandmother's face the last time she had seen it, all lit up at the sight of the workers.

Ella and Adrian barely knew what was happening as people came and went and shook hands and told the family they were sorry for their loss. Everyone was very kind, and a mix of the local friends were pouring tea and handing out sandwiches. Ella could hardly remember what had happened once the day was over. She didn't know whom she had spoken to, or what she had said. She was just about there. The second day of the wake, she went up to her room around four pm to try and get away from the people for a short time. She lay on her bed and shut her eyes, the voices downstairs travelling up to her, sounding like they were underwater. When her mum came up to check on her, it was six pm and she had slept.

'Where were you?'

'I just went up to have a rest and accidentally fell asleep.'

'Ryley was worried about you. Come down when you're ready.' Her mum walked over to her and gave her a kiss on the forehead, pushing her hair back. 'It's been tough, I know.'

Ella nodded. 'It has. How are you holding up?'

Her mum shrugged. 'I don't know yet. Ask me in a few days when the wake and the funeral are over.'

Ella gave her mum a hug and got up and redid her hair. She was wearing a skirt for the first time since she had told her parents she had left, and it was creased. She went over to her wardrobe to look for another one. When she opened the door, her eyes fell on a diary she had kept from when she was younger. She grabbed a skirt and took out the diary. As she was getting changed, she read a couple of lines of the diary.

10 December 2005

Dear diary, today I made my choice to serve God. I am very happy with this choice and I know that God will keep me until the end. The worker told me to read the Bible and pray every morning and every evening. I will give it a go, but I know that I am not good at doing things every day. Mum tells me I need to brush my teeth every day, and I am not brilliant at that so we will see. I do know that this is very important, though, so I will do my best. I hear mum calling us to have a cup of hot chocolate. Will talk soon!
Ella x

14 December 2005

Dear diary, it has been four days since I made my choice. I have already forgotten to read my Bible and pray twice. I feel very bad about this, I will try to do better in the coming days. Today I told my friend Grainne that I professed. I

have told her about the meetings, but she thinks she may be an atheist, which means she doesn't believe in God. I hope she will change her mind or she will go to a lost eternity. We are going to eat at Granny and Grandad's house this evening. I hope it won't be too boring. They wouldn't let us read books the last time so we had to play board games with them. They made me BORED. Anyway, I need to go!
    Ella x

Ella placed the diary back on the shelf. It was weird thinking back to that time when she had believed everything the workers told them. She didn't have the mental energy to think about it right now, though, so she pushed the thought of it back down and went back downstairs. She saw Ryley talking to some of her old friends and went over to them.

The next day was the same, except she'd slept a bit more during the night. The funeral was the next day, Sunday, so they were given a rundown at breakfast time and told about the hall and who the workers would be. It would be in the afternoon, shortly after people had eaten and before the mission. Timothy would be speaking at the grave, much to four people's disgust, and the rest's surprise and delight.

The morning of the funeral, there was no meeting, so the kids all went for a walk to clear their heads. Justin ran on ahead with the dog that Anna and Peter had got after Ella left home. They walked as a group, the couples holding hands.

'How are we all doing?' Harry said, his voice sombre.

'Shit. My granny has died and some of her last words to me were about how she hates my relationship. Also, Timothy is speaking at her funeral, just to finish it off nicely.'

They filed into the silent hall at quarter to one. The funeral would start at one. They sat in the first two rows. Harry got sent to the back.

'I'm sorry, but I can't have people talking on top of everything,' Anna whispered to Adrian when she told Harry to move. Ella saw her brother's fists ball up, but he didn't say anything.

'It's so unfair, I'm so sorry. Do you want me to tell Mum to quit the BS?' she whispered quietly to him.

'No. Just leave it for now.'

She didn't reply, just looked at him.

'Seriously, leave it. I don't want to make it worse.'

She left it. When the worker stood up to welcome them all, the three outcasts sat like there was nothing weird about being back in what was essentially a meeting.

'We are all gathered here to remember the loss of our servant, Patricia. The loss of Patricia, a faithful soul, will be deeply felt by all here, but especially her ...'

Ella's mind was already starting to wander. She knew that this would be the only bit of the funeral that addressed the fact that her grandmother had lived a life outside of being a member of the two-by-twos.

As predicted, the funeral turned into what was essentially a gospel meeting, no doubt intended for the four non-professing people in attendance, the 'lost sheep,' as they were referred to at their own grandmother's funeral.

Ella shifted in her chair as the worker opened the Bible and read a verse about something that Jesus had done. Ryley nudged her softly, showing her the words he had added to the hymn sheet that they had been given. They changed the words of the hymns into something that was actually quite wholesome – the meaning had been about sacrificing your life for the cause, but now it spoke about the love that people could have for themselves and others. They showed it to Adrian and he smiled. Once the worker had finished speaking, the prayer was over, and the two chosen groups of men had lifted the coffin down the street for a short while, Adrian fell into step beside Ryley, Ella, and Harry, and asked for the piece of paper back.

'That's all that they really need here,' he said quietly, not wanting to be overhead. 'More love, less judgement, and then *all* of the issues that we have would be replaced. There's this fake love that they give.' He was waving the piece of paper as he spoke.

Ella nodded.

'They did give us a lot of help recently to be fair.'

'Yes, but they also judged us heavily, spoke behind our backs, I heard them. Obviously not all of them, but there are enough of them that are so focused on the wrong things, it ruins the whole group.'

They stood at the graveside, watching the small coffin of their grandmother be set down. The people around the grave were silent. The birds around the grave still singing away. Harry stood beside Adrian this time, not touching him but just being a support for him as he wasn't allowed to be in the undertaker's hall. The people standing around shifted in the cold air as Timothy, the man the four had lost all respect for, took the microphone and prayed at the graveside of their grandmother. Ella couldn't help but think that that man had stolen enough of her last few moments with her granny so it was fitting that he would be ruining the last ones before she would be lowered to the ground.

They all stared at the ground as Timothy prayed for the lost souls.

'Hey, we're famous,' Ella whispered just loud enough for Ryley and Adrian to hear, both of whom giggled.

She had seen her friend Hannah in a long skirt with her hair in a bun and was feeling weird. She was sad about her grandmother, but also felt strange about seeing her friend in the clothing of someone who looked as though they were in a cult.

When Timothy was eventually finished and the coffin was lowered into the ground, they were all freezing. But they still had to hug or shake hands with all the people that had come. They stood lined up as many people passed them.

When Hannah came along the line, she asked Ella if they could chat at the hotel afterwards. Ella nodded and smiled at her, but it felt odd knowing that her friend had taken a completely different path to her in life. Things were normal with Grace, who Ella knew supported her no matter what. It was just with Hannah, whom she had known her whole life, that things felt weird.

In the car on the way to the hotel, things were slightly lighter.

'Man, that brought it all back,' Adrian commented, putting his arm around Harry in the back, giving his boyfriend a quick kiss on the lips.

'You're telling me. I felt like I was in the closet again today. I need to do very gay things to you tonight.'

'Ew, that's my brother you're talking to,' Ella protested, glancing at them via the rear-view mirror. She smiled when she saw them, though. They made a cute couple.

'Yeah man, that's also very gay of you both,' Ryley added. They laughed.

'But seriously, lads, I have to tell my parents that how they treated me with the whole case is not okay. They literally allowed Timothy, the man who arranged for me to see Fred face to face, to pray at the graveside of my grandmother. I'm not even that surprised with how they treat us for being gay, but that is where I draw the line. They need to know how their reactions to it affected me, too.'

'Yeah, I agree. Leave it a short while for them to get over the loss, but we should definitely have a conversation with them about that.'

The others agreed.

At the hotel, Ella joined the line for the food, just ending up beside Hannah and Grace, who were chatting.

'Hey, Ella! How are you doing? Sorry about your granny.'

She nodded and smiled awkwardly, as she had so many times already.

'Yeah, well, it was fast and relatively painless, and you know, she had had a long life,' Ella said as she had so often the last couple of days after hearing it enough times from others.

'Yeah, she has gone on to a better place at least,' Hannah said. 'So, how are things with you, Hannah? They put you in the small but scary Donegal.'

'Hardly small,' Hannah laughed, 'yeah things are good, you know we had a few people going out to the meetings recently. A young couple and an older man.'

Ella nodded, letting the words float past her.

'Are you happy, though?' They were almost at the buffet.

'I'm so happy. I just know I'm in my place.' The glazed expression was switched on, so Ella just let her talk. Grace was genuinely interested in what she was saying, and Ella was happy to see her friend in a good enough place, but it was not fun knowing that she no longer had as much in common with her best friend. It was as though Grace believed that Hannah was on a higher level than her – the strange the effect it had on the two-by-twos when someone became a worker.

Ella had to go to sit with her family, so the conversation came to an end. She put her plate down and gave both of her friends a quick hug.

'Thanks so much for coming. I really love you both.'

As she walked away, she felt somehow sadder about that conversation than she had felt since she'd initially heard about her grandmother's passing. It felt like she had lost Hannah, even though she was still alive. She was just in a different ideology to Ella. Ella sighed and sat down beside her boyfriend, one of the stable points in her life right now. She gave him a quick kiss.

'What was that for?' He laughed.

'Just 'cause I love you so much.'

It was weird, Ella found, processing a loss with the safety net of seeing your relative in heaven. She was okay with it, but it was strange. It felt like she had to rethink ways to accept it, which added another layer to the process.

Chapter Twenty

Adrian sat opposite his parents at the dinner table. Ella and Ryley were on either side, supporting him in their own ways. Justin had been sent to his friend's house. He didn't need to be here for this.

'Mum, Dad,' Adrian started, 'I love you both, but there is something really important that I haven't been straightforward about. There are a couple of things actually. As you know, I have left the meetings because of the actions of Fred. Your original response to me telling the police was incredibly hurtful to me, and I carry the weight of your lack of support with me every day.'

Anna looked shocked. Peter's expression was closed off.

'I was probably at my most vulnerable that day. I thought it was my own fault that Fred had abused me, and all you guys did was cement that feeling. I have another friend within the friends, who was telling me about their own experience of abuse as a child, and do you know what their parents did when they told them?'

Anna and Peter shook their heads.

'They supported them, they went to the head workers about it, and they told the kid that if she wanted to go to the police, that they would support that entirely. They didn't want their daughter to suffer for one moment more.' Adrian paused, breathing heavily.

'And guess what? It was still a super hard experience for that girl. She still had a lot to go through even though her parents stood behind her every step of the way – of course she did. You know why? It's because this is such a hard situation to be in. That girl, she isn't in Ireland by the way, but she has been stopped at so many points as she has gone to the police about her situation. She has had to fight tooth and nail to bring the case to the court. As have I. Just to try to bring a rapist to justice.'

Anna shivered slightly at the word.

'Yes mum, a rapist,' Ella said. Adrian nodded.

'We can't shy away from using the word. You know, I have debated so many times whether I wanted to even bring this up with you. Everything that we have been taught by you and by the workers is to forgive and forget, no matter the crime. But I am so fed up with that line of thought. It just allows people to push forward and commit the crimes without having to worry about the consequences. Yes, perfect way, imperfect people, etc etc etc. We know. But the imperfect people are allowed by the "perfect way" to get away with it and continue their "imperfect actions" more and more. The whole setup is wrong. Look, it isn't just your faults. We know that you were doing the best you could. But you didn't try to step in at that crucial point. You just said, well, he can figure it out himself, and turned your back on me. You listened to Timothy more than you listened to your own son. All I need from you both at this point is an acknowledgement that you were wrong to do it, an apology and we can move on from it. Provided of course that you change your response if anyone else, like Ella or Justin, were to come to you with the same issue, or even one of your siblings, or even each other because it can happen to anyone. Or even your future grandchildren – you never know. Now I sincerely hope, from the bottom of my heart, that no one in our family ever has to go through what I went through. That you would listen to them, validate their experience, and support them if they went to the police. Can you do that for me? Apologise, acknowledge, and do better?'

Anna and Peter looked at each other. The tears were streaming down Anna's face.

'I can't believe you would all gang up on us like this,' Anna sniffed.

'Mum. This is not about you. This is not an attack on you as parents. Stop with twisting it. Just stop. We acknowledge that this is hard to hear, but we need you to focus on what is important right now.'

Anna started crying even harder.

'I can't believe how incredibly unfeeling you are all being towards your mum right now. I want all of you out of my home, right now!' Peter shouted.

The three turned to each other.

'What do you want to do now?' Ella asked Adrian.

'I want to sit here and face them,' Adrian replied, stony faced.

They nodded and turned to the parents.

'We aren't going to leave the house, Dad.' Ella's voice shook as she said it, but she kept going. 'If you want to go to another room to gather your emotions, we understand. If you need a walk, we understand. Collect yourselves, but we are finishing this discussion one way or another today if possible.'

Peter's face grew redder as she spoke, but he nodded and took his wife by the arm and they marched out of the house, slamming the door behind them.

They drew a collective sigh of relief when the door was shut.

'How are you holding up?' Ryley asked both of them.

'I am still sitting here which is against every sliver of my being. But I just wish it were over.'

Ella nodded.

'Yeah, I completely understand. I—' She broke off as Adrian stood up and ran out to the toilet, where they heard him retching.

Ella followed him out.

'Hey, are you okay?' She knocked on the door. Stupid thing to ask. Few people are okay when they're throwing up. There was a moment's pause before his voice, weak in stark contrast to how strong it had been, spoke.

'It's so hard. I feel like I'm being the adult here and they are acting like I'm the one in the wrong. Just for speaking my truth.'

'Yeah. It isn't fair.'

'No, it's not fucking fair.' He retched again, and she gave him some time.

When he came back out, she gave him a hug.

'Hey, not so tight or I'll treat you the way I treated that toilet.'

She half smiled and loosened her grip.

'We are all here for you, Adrian.'

She squeezed him again and they walked back into the kitchen, arm-in-arm.

'You okay, Adrian?'

'I'll be okay, thanks Ry.'

They sat at the table in silence.

After a while, the door opened, and the three of them looked up. Anna and Peter walked in and sat down.

'We have had a think about what you said, Adrian.'

'We were wrong to not support you more.' They were playing the united front, Ella observed.

'We know that your points are valid. But we also think that you have been spending too much time on the internet, which is of course full of negative things about this way. If you delved deeper into the way—'

'Get to the point,' Adrian interrupted.

'Look, we are sorry, and we would go back and do it differently if we could,' Peter admitted. 'Even with how we treated you about your relationship.'

'Thanks.'

'And we want to be more supportive of you always, but especially for the next while,' Anna added. 'We know it won't be easy as the case goes on, but we are here for you.'

'I really appreciate that, Mum. But why did you both just push it away when I told you both?'

They looked at each other.

'We didn't want to believe it,' Peter said, after a brief pause. 'We have heard of other things happening, to other people, but that is something you can kind of ignore, if you know what I mean? Like I could put it in another box, but then when you came and said all those things, it was too real. I wanted you to stop telling me those things. I don't know about you, Anna, but I just … I just pushed it out of my head, said that you were lying, because the alternative hurt. It hurt a lot, too much.'

Peter, their tough dad, who always faced everything stoically, was crying. Ella didn't know how to process that.

'I appreciate your honesty, Dad. Can you imagine, though, how much more painful it was for me? First I had the trauma itself, and then I had to go through you both not even supporting me.'

'I wanted to.' Anna spoke quietly, looking down at her hands. They all turned to look at her.

'When you started behaving weirdly, all those years ago, I had wondered. I saw my little boy turn into a confused mess. I asked Fred if anything had happened, because I knew you had spent some time together. He denied anything out of the ordinary happening, and I didn't want to think of the alternative, so I left it.' Her voice was shaking. 'When you came to us,' she continued, 'all I could think about was how I hadn't pushed him further, harder, to tell me. I felt so guilty about not having protected you.' She was crying, along with Ella and Adrian. Even Peter had tears running down his face.

'In my guilt, I pushed you away.' Anna took a deep breath, her hands shaking as she touched her face, attempting to stem the flow of the tears. 'I sent you off to college, brought you there with Ella, and felt nothing. I had pushed my love of my own son down, in an attempt to try and protect myself.'

Ryley stood up and grabbed some tissues, passing them around the room and grabbing some for himself.

'I haven't slept properly for a year. Your dad will vouch for me – I have been like a tigress.'

Peter nodded, and they all let out a collective chuckle.

'Adrian, I am your mother. I birthed you. At the end of the day, your pain is my pain, and I have felt that pain so intensely, so raw. I love you more than life itself and I will never not regret what happened to you and that I did not step in to stop that monster. I should have told you to go to the guards.' She stood up, and the soaking tissues fell to the floor. She walked over to her son and embraced him. He stood up and hugged her back.

'I'm so so so sorry,' she said, over and over again.

Peter stood up and joined their embrace. 'I'm sorry, too.'

They stood like that, the three of them, and then Anna held her arms out to Ella. Ella took Ryley's hand and brought him in to the embrace, too. They all stood, in a tight circle, and felt the pain of it all, letting the agony of the last years seep through their bodies and out in the form of tears.

Chapter Twenty-One

Three years later

They stood outside the courtroom, dressed in their smartest clothes. Harry, Ella, and Ryley stood on one side of Adrian, with Justin, Anna, and Peter on the other.

'Are you ready?' Ella turned to Adrian.

'I think so.'

It had been a long few years. When the decision had been made to bring the case to trial, Fred was thankfully in the country, as he had said he would be. It was the only thing he had fully gone along with. He had denied all claims initially, and it had seemed that it wouldn't even be able to go any further, but at the last moment, three other victims had come forward. Adrian had been lucky, he knew. Most victims within the friends never wanted to report it, meaning it looked like it wasn't going to go anywhere – either because of their own fear, or because they were told by others not to. Adrian knew this, as he had slowly heard of more victims (and his heart had sunk every time a new one came forward), and he had asked each one he had heard about, in person, if they would consider testifying. It was looking desperate, when another man of his age, and two women a little younger than him, came forward and testified.

There was a collective sigh of relief when Adrian got the call on a Friday afternoon from the case manager. When they were eventually informed of the court case, they were told that Fred had been released on bail. They didn't have to go to the first few hearings, but he had been called a couple of times to testify as a witness, which Harry had accompanied him to each time. Today he would read his statement of impact, and then the court would be open to the public.

This was hopefully their last court date, though. All of the evidence had been presented and the jury was, all being well, going to give its decision.

They walked up the steps together. Ella and Ryley had got married just a month prior, and were just back from their honeymoon. They had lived together for a year while they were engaged, and then they got married when they were both finished their studies. Harry and Adrian were living together in Dublin, where they were both working. Harry was a solicitor, and Adrian was a mental health nurse, having changed his study after a year. After many years of being together, the pair planned to get married in a few years. Justin had also left the meetings, leaving their parents with their last hope for the meetings gone. They had become a lot more open-minded in the meantime, though, putting their kids first. And Justin, as far as Ella knew, was sleeping around as he studied to be a vet.

When the family was allowed into the court, they took their places beside Adrian, who was sitting in the middle of the section dedicated to the public. Ella, sitting on one side of him, took his hand, and Harry took the other. When everything was settled, the jury gave its decision to the judge.

Adrian could hardly hear the lead up to the decision. It seemed as though the words were coming from far, far away.

'Guilty on all charges' suddenly seeped through.

'Did I hear that right?' Adrian turned to Harry. 'Did they find him guilty?'

Harry nodded, his face breaking into a broad grin.

'He has been found guilty.'

The judge sentenced Fred to ten years in prison for his crimes. When all the proceedings were finished, Adrian watched Fred be taken away in handcuffs with mixed feelings. He had brought the case to the police to help prevent further issues for those with whom Fred came in contact, and he was proud of himself for that, but the choice of the court wasn't something he was overly happy with. He wished that Fred would have been put behind bars for life, as he knew that in ten years, Fred would be back out. And it might even end up shorter, the guards had warned.

Adrian didn't voice his concerns immediately, as he wanted to enjoy the feeling of satisfaction and achievement first. He had done it. He had stood up against a whole organisation, and he had won.

They walked as a family arm-in-arm towards the car, united. *They* had won.

Acknowledgements

First and foremost, I want to thank my life partner, for being there for me as I went through the process of first leaving, and then deciding to write about it. It has not been an easy journey, but I am glad to have you by my side every step of the way. I would also like to thank those family members that know about the book, you know who you are. I am so grateful to you all for your unconditional support and love. I love you all.

To my editor, Claire Strombeck, who shaped this book into what it is. Without Claire, this book would have been half of what it is and pretty unreadable.

To all of those friends who encouraged me, and acted as guinea pigs as I threw the roughest drafts at you. I appreciate you all. To those friends I don't even know in person who have helped me limp along the journey, I am indebted to you all. To those who listened to my story and assured me it was interesting enough to write about, I appreciate it.

To every person who shaped me into the person I am today, allowing me to turn simple individual words into a story. Thank you.